BLESSED
MARIE-CELINE
OF THE PRESENTATION

*"Being made perfect in a
short space, he fulfilled a
long time."* —Wisdom 4:13

Blessed Marie Celine of the Presentation, who died in the odor
of sanctity on the 30th of May, 1897, at the age of 19, in the
Monastery of the Poor Clares of Bordeaux—Talence (France),
now at Nieul Sur Mer (France). Although Bl. Marie Celine
made her religious profession on her deathbed and thus
received a black veil, portraits usually show her wearing the
white veil of a novice.

BLESSED MARIE-CELINE
OF THE PRESENTATION

(Germaine Castang)
1878-1897
Poor Clare Nun of Bordeaux-Talence, France

Translated and Compiled by the
Poor Clares of Rockford, Illinois

"For thou hast done man-
fully, and thy heart has been
strengthened." (Judith 15:11)

TAN BOOKS AND PUBLISHERS, INC.
Rockford, Illinois 61105

Nihil Obstat: Reverend Monsignor David D. Kagan, J.C.L.
Vicar General, Diocese of Rockford

Imprimatur: Reverend Monsignor David D. Kagan, J.C.L.
Vicar General, Diocese of Rockford
Rockford, Illinois
May 7, 2007

This book was compiled from several sources: Part One—an anonymous and undated French book entitled *Soeur Marie-Celine de la Présentation (Germaine Castang): Clarisse 1878-1897* that was published by Poor Clares in France and translated by the Poor Clares of Rockford, Illinois; Part Two— from excerpts from *Sister Marie-Céline of the Presentation: "A Lily of the Cloister,"* by Rev. J. A. Shields, published with Imprimatur by St. Anselm's Priory, Washington, D.C., 1928, copyright 1928 The Benedictine Foundation at Washington, and used with permission of the Foundation; Part Three— from a translation of the *"Lettres inédites de Soeur Céline, provenant du monastère des Clarisses des Pessac,"* présentées par Jeanne Briand, as published in approximately 1997 by Monastere de Fontaudin-Pessac in a book entitled *Marie Céline de Nojals à Pessac: 1878-1897: Clarisse*; Part Four— from selections from *Graces and Favours: A Record of Heavenly Favours attributed to the Powerful Intercession of Sister Marie-Céline, Poor Clare, American Edition—No. 2,* edited and published with Imprimatur in approximately 1926 by Giovanni Serpentelli, Streatham Hall, Exter, on behalf of The Poor Clares of Mons, Belgium (All rights reserved); Part Five—photos of the Colettine Poor Clares of Corpus Christi Monastery, Rockford, Illinois.

ISBN-10: 0-89555-845-9
ISBN-13: 978-0-89555-845-9

Printed and bound in the United States of America.

TAN BOOKS AND PUBLISHERS, INC.
P.O. Box 424
Rockford, Illinois 61105
2007

Dedication

To the young women of our time
whom God is calling to follow the Lamb
with courage and generosity.
May their love be strong, and may its impulse
lead them to offer themselves
as willing victims for the salvation of souls.

*With courageous heart she followed the Lamb
Who was crucified for love of us;
she offered herself as a chaste and spotless victim."
—Antiphon from the Common of Virgins,
Liturgy of the Hours*

Germaine Castang in her school uniform shortly before entering the Poor Clare monastery; she is wearing the blue ribbon of a Child of Mary. We are indebted to Germaine's father for this picture; he required her to have herself photographed before he would give his consent to her entry into the convent.

Words of
Cardinal Bourne

*(From the Preface to a biography of Sister Marie Celine
that was published in 1923.)**

AT THE request of the Abbess of the Convent of
Poor Clares formerly at Talence near Bordeaux,
and now in exile in Belgium [during World
War I], I gladly write these few words of commenda-
tion of the English version of the life of their holy sister, Marie-Céline, who died with a high reputation for
sanctity in 1897 at the age of nineteen.

God has been pleased in these later days to mani-
fest in a special way to the world the essential simplicity of holiness, attained by close union with Him,
in the perfect performance of the most ordinary duties
of the way of life to which a soul has been called. Such
was the life of the Blessed Teresa of the Child Jesus,
the wonderful little Carmelite whose virtues the Church
is publicly recognizing at this moment when we write.
Of similar calling and attainment would seem to be
the Poor Clare Sister Marie-Céline of the Presentation, the story of whose short life is now given to us
in English. There are many others, some only known
in the intimacy of the family or of the cloister to which
they belonged, others the fame of whose virtue is gradually becoming known more widely.

These lives have surely an immense significance for

---

* *Sister Celine: Poor Clare, Or Abridged Life of Sister Marie-Céline
of the Presentation, "A Lily of the Cloister"* . . . , Written by a
Poor Clare, Abridged from the French Life by R.B.M. Foster (London: Burns Oates and Washbourne Ltd.), 1923.

all, both in religion and in the world; and they will most certainly be a powerful encouragement to the innumerable souls whom God is constantly inviting to closer union with Himself, not by wonderful or striking deed, but by humble, persevering and untiring endeavour to accomplish with unfailing fidelity the tasks, be they easy or very hard, that constitute for each one of us the God-appointed path that we have individually to tread in order to attain the object for which we have been placed upon this earth. May this Life, now made available for English readers, be a fresh source of courage to all who are earnestly seeking God.

FRANCIS CARDINAL BOURNE
Archbishop of Westminster

Compilers' Note

THE present book in its English translation is a compilation of several French publications about the life of Sister Marie Celine of the Presentation, P.C.C., sent to us by our Poor Clare Sisters in Pessac, France, who were the privileged custodians of her mortal remains. These materials we have translated and edited with the kind assistance of Mr. Gustave Gilg and finally combined into a single book.

This young Colettine Poor Clare, though little known, is one of the giants of the "little way" and has often been compared to her contemporary, St. Therese of Lisieux. We present her story to the English-speaking world as an example of heroism and humility which we look up to and for which we give thanks to God.

Any favors received through the intercession of Blessed Marie Celine of the Presentation may be made known to any of the following. (See p. 153 for websites and phone numbers.)

The Poor Clare Nuns
Corpus Christi Monastery
2111 South Main Street
Rockford, IL 61102-3591

The Poor Clare Nuns
Annunciation Monastery
6200 East Minooka Rd.
Minooka, IL 60447-9458

Monastere Ste. Claire
2, Avenue de la Rochelle
17137 NIEUL SUR MER
France

A. Vanderpl., Braine—Iallend

Authentic portrait of Blessed Marie-Celine
of the Presentation, Poor Clare.
Beatification, September 16, 2007.
"In Heaven I will forget no one . . ."—Bl. Marie Celine.

Foreword

Taken from the French edition of Part One

THIS is the brief history of a life without relief, of a life constantly wounded, which came to completion in its early springtime. The story is told in modest terms which well match the poverty of the heroine.

The minute I wrote the word, I hesitated to use it, for it seems too big for the littleness of the young girl who is the subject of these pages. A heroine is, after all, according to our most rigorous dictionaries, a "woman of great courage, who proves by her conduct in exceptional circumstances to have a strength of soul above the average." It seems that in the present case this would be saying too much, since Sr. Celine's existence did not know exceptional circumstances.

What is less exceptional or more banal than poverty, defeat, rebuffs, humiliations, sadness and illness? That was precisely the course of this short life, in which suffering alone seems to stand out, inflicting incessant trials. But to have strength of soul above average when life is nothing but suffering: that is even more exceptional than rare circumstances, especially when this strength is manifested since infancy in a being as fragile as was this Poor Clare of 19 years.

Those who wish to know whence Sr. Celine draws her energy and joy will discover it in reading these pages. The story is always the same: the strength of God reveals itself and is displayed in the feebleness of the humble.

Fr. Barthelemy Laboirie, Franciscan
Minister Provincial of Aquitaine

Introduction

Taken from the French edition of Part One

GOD has given to our century Saints without miracles, without interventions in public affairs: people like any others, to whom nothing draws attention.

Here is a little country girl whose life is spent in the kitchen of her paternal home, then in an orphanage, and who dies at the age of 19 in a Poor Clare monastery.

Before such a sequence of events, this question arises: What did she do, this little one? Here the workings of grace stand isolated, showing forth, one could say, the mechanism, the technique of sanctification.

This biography will be only *"the story of a soul."* Celine was a contemporary of Therese of Lisieux. The two Sisters died the same year, a few months apart, both dying prematurely in the cloister, sanctified by *"the heroism of little things."*

The little Saint, Therese, formulated the doctrine of *"spiritual childhood"* which was the fruit of her own experience. Sr. Celine only lived it. She wrote nothing, she did not analyze herself. We have from her hand but a few poor letters and the notes of a retreat, in a clumsy style—in which one can nevertheless find some very beautiful things.

Her life, on the other hand, was quite dramatic: this child knew some astonishing afflictions. The characteristics of this humble and lofty soul were clearly a strength of soul which confounded and an admirable self-forgetfulness.

And on top of such pain and generosity there blossomed, like a flower opening to the morning, divine love. This young girl is a master of the ideal.

—Fr. Martial Lekeux, Franciscan

Contents

PART ONE

The Life of Sister Marie Celine

❧ Chapter 1 ❧

At Home

The Castang Family

A T DAWN on May 23, 1878, in the village of Nojals in Dordogne, France, the home of Germain Castang welcomed its fifth "blessing," as these Christians expressed it. The child, inscribed in the civil registers under the name of "Emilie-Julie," received at Baptism the name of "Jeanne." But her father, according to a very curious custom of the country, gave her a third name, and so she who was to die under the name of "Sister Celine" was in Nojals called nothing but "Germaine," or "little Maine."

Three brothers and a sister preceded her: Louis, who was nine years old at Germaine's birth, Lucie, Guilbert and Levy, the last named being born the year before. The family, which in the end was to number twelve children, at that time lived in a large house facing the church which the father himself had built.

The Castangs were considered upright people, but they were soft of heart. Native to Nojals, her father, Germain, belonged to this bubbly "gasconne" race and he personified the typical Frenchman—dark and stocky, lively, very rough and hard working, but proud, very

3

personable and easily excited. He did not have any one trade. This robust man, enterprising and resourceful, was capable, after all, of performing more than one job, but he did so with a lack of spirit which ended in disaster. This fault did not prevent him from being congenial, for he was thoroughly good, upright and particularly generous.

In juxtaposition to this rich but inconstant temperament, his older brother, Etienne, was poised, balanced and stable in his enterprises. He lived on the paternal farm, which he directed all his life long.

At 23, Germain married Marie Lafage, who was 17. She was from Saint-Avit-Senieur, born into what one calls "a good family": one of her ancestors was the notary of the village. Her father was addressed as "Moussu" or "Mouchu," and she herself as "Madomegelle"—titles which in the country indicate a certain social rank. Her reserve, her unalterable calm, contrasted with the exuberance of Germain. The striking thing about Marie was the happy combination of sweetness and firmness which one finds in profound souls.

The young spouses were made to complement one another. They had in common two magnificent characteristics: they were both marked with goodness, that is, with big hearts, capable of dealing out charity unto ultimate self-sacrifice; and above all, they possessed in the depths of their souls a strong faith, comprehensive and firm as a rock.

In such a Christian milieu, the Castangs were defined by their fervor: Marie having a more lively piety, but both spouses being uncompromising in their principles.

The young family made its abode in what would be called a "pigeon hole," a small elevated building in the

middle of the fields, about a hundred meters from the village. As the family grew, Germain sold the pigsty, bought a small plot in the village and built the house in which the family celebrated the birth of *little Maine.*
The village of Nojals numbered about 250 people, most of them scattered throughout the countryside, the rest occupying the town, which was composed of about fifteen houses grouped around the church. The "main street" in the village was a path which passed by the church and branched off in two directions after a curve. Between the two branches of the fork were the school and a few houses, as well as a tiny town hall under the huge linden trees that shaded the path to the church. At one end of the village was located the Castang farm, occupied at that time by "Uncle Etienne"; at the other end was the bridge over the Bournegue, a stream that irrigated the region.

It was between the paths, at the level of the church, that Germain Castang built his new home. On account of the sloping terrain, the building had, on one side of the street, a ground floor, and above, a first floor, which was accessible from the side facing the church through the garden on the top level. To increase the family's income, there was set up on the ground floor a small grocery store with a cafe and a pool table.

The family lived on the first floor. As with all country homes, the vast kitchen was the main room where the family ordinarily gathered, either around the long table or at the hearth, where a slow wood fire burned.

The windows opened to the church on one side and, on the other, looked out upon the beautiful countryside with its fields of wheat, clover and corn, beyond which were the wooded hills. At the foot of these, between the poplars, was the winding Bournegue. Such was the overall appearance of this fertile region, with its discreet charm that gave an impression of the happiness and peace in a simple country life.

Germaine's Early Life

It was in this rustic and strong environment that the humble girl grew up, she who one day was to become so beautiful before God and men.

This supernatural beauty was above all the work of her mother. This is a frequent fact in hagiography. There is nothing astonishing in this: a mother forms her child.

Upon questioning those who knew "La Faguette," as Marie was called, one always received the same answer: "Madame Castang was a saint." All agreed in praising her piety, her courage at work, her great common sense, a charity which some thought excessive and an admirable valor under trial.

When Germaine learned how to speak, her mother taught her the *Pater* and the *Ave* and some dear little prayers that rhymed, which were a family tradition. I cannot resist the temptation to transcribe the prayer which Lubine, a younger sister of Germaine, recited for me without a hitch at 60 years of age and with visible pleasure.

Our Father in Heaven, Father of all the world, it is You who take care of Your little children. But to such goodness You wish us to respond and to ask for Your graces for our loved ones. I implore You for those whom I love, for the Church and the Holy Father, for France, for sinners and for the suffering souls.

The prayer is simple, unsophisticated, but full of meaning; and one should note the altruistic character of these invocations; we can learn much from children to think of others in praying.

That which Germaine saw all around her was a modest life, taken up entirely with work. Her father worked hard. As for Madame Castang, if she was not at prayer, she was at her duty: six children (a little brother followed Germaine but did not live long), the household and, in the absence of her husband, the running of the store and the serving of the customers. The valiant mother went from one task to another, active and calm, always smiling because all was done for God and her children.

Very early, Germaine could watch her sister Lucie, five years her senior, who already helped her mother with the household chores. Expenses began to increase, and Uncle Etienne took Lucie to live with his family in order to alleviate his brother's situation. Germaine no longer saw her big sister except from time to time, and as soon as she was knee-high, she hastened to do her best to replace Lucie at her mother's side.

In all of this, the child learned from her own parents some magnificent lessons in charity. There was also this tradition in her family: that all the needy were sure to find shelter and a bed for the night. The house was the refuge of all the indigents of the region.

One day, when Mr. Castang had already given to several beggars, another asked for help. A visiting relative, feeling that the beggar was exaggerating his need, sent him away. Mr. Castang was no sooner told of this than he said to Lucie as he held out a coin: "Here, run after him and give this to him." And he added: "One is never impoverished by giving a *sou* to a poor man."

On another occasion, the door opened to a woman in rags in the frozen rain who held in her arms a child in tatters and trembling from the cold. The heart of Madame Castang could not hold out, and she quickly let the poor things in, sat them by the fire and ran to her closet. She clothed mother and child in her very best, restored their strength and sent them on their way comforted.

There was nothing superfluous in that home. The couple was barely able to meet their needs, but they believed firmly in the duty of charity. They gave as much as they could give, depriving themselves in order to help others.

The charity of the Castangs was spoken of even in the nearby villages. It was talked about among the family . . . and it was also criticized. However, would to God that more Christians could merit so honorable a reproach! If Germain Castang ended in ruin, it was for reasons other than his alms.

At four years of age, little Maine was a delightful child, with her big blue-green eyes and her fixed gaze, blond ringlets and pretty angel face, always smiling. Passersby would return to say: "Oh, what a beautiful child!" She was the favorite, though no one was jealous.

At that time Germaine went to the Sisters' nursery, about a hundred feet from the house. She also accompanied her mother to church, attending all the Masses, and deriving from this contact the attraction to prayer which later marked her life so distinctly.

Nevertheless, all children have within themselves a little monster, and parents recognize the early appearance of tiny faults which need only time in order to become real vices. Germaine was a Castang: she did have faults which needed to be conquered. She was terribly willful—sometimes violently so, of an excessive sensitivity, and above all, like all children, mischievous. She did not delay in showing that she had character. One day, after having eaten a sardine without touching her bread, Germaine asked for a second. As she was refused, she snapped back this impertinent little remark: "Well, then! I will go around saying your sardines are no good, and then you won't sell any more. There!" Needless to say, the scolding was immediate, and she was forever cured of such remarks.

On another day, having been given permission to go to the patronal feast of Beaumont with one of her brothers, Germaine had a passionate desire to see the puppet show there. The show was at a late hour, but Germaine announced, "I want to see the puppet show. We are staying!" Having thus silenced the voice of her conscience and led astray her brother, she enjoyed the forbidden fruit. When the two knocked on the door of their house, it was one o'clock in the morning. Mr. Castang opened to them, not without a sharp reprimand—but that was only the half of it. When they heard the voice of their mother threatening to intervene, the little delinquents were struck with panic and fled to their room. They gained nothing by stalling, though, and in the morning a just punishment reminded them of the meaning of duty.

This strictness, always judicious in correcting, was tempered by a habitual goodness and sweetness which made the children accept deserved reprimands willingly.

These childish incidents of a little saint are very opportune lessons in our age which encourages parents to neglect the sacred function of disciplining their children, a duty which is laid upon them in order to form the future.

Suffering Enters Germaine's Life

The Castang couple did their best to raise their children in a Christian manner, though not all would be sanctified in the same way.

Little Maine was four years old when she received the first touch of the Master. She was then the charming child which has been described: so lively, gay and exuberant, a budding blossom, and passionate for life. Already God was calling her to share in His austere joys.

One day the child left school with some of her companions, and the clamorous little troop headed toward the bridge over the Bournegue. One little girl had the idea of going in to wade, and soon the whole band was splashing around in the stream. Germaine had done like the others. The water was ice cold, but that is not what made this intrepid little girl draw back. The intervention of a passerby put an end to the party. But, alas, it was too late! The little one had left her good health behind in that stream.

Soon after arriving home, Germaine fell into a bizarre drowsiness. The following day, when she arrived at school, she curled up on the floor and immediately fell asleep. For three days she did nothing but sleep. When she was awakened and questioned about it, she could only answer, "My legs hurt," and fall back into a deep sleep. Alarmed, her parents sent for the doctor. He tried to help but soon her left leg became paralyzed and her foot deformed. It swelled and became monstrous. The doctor admitted his powerlessness.

Gracious little Maine had become no more than a cripple. This was bitter for her—and for her poor parents. Heartbroken at seeing their favorite little one withering away before their eyes, they multiplied prayers and novenas, begging Heaven to have pity on themselves and on their child.

At some 1500 meters from the village, in the hamlet of Clottes, there was an ancient chapel dedicated to St. Anne. It was customary to make a pilgrimage there on the feast of the Saint. Madame Castang resolved to go that year to ask Good St. Anne, who was also a mother, for the cure of her child.

But Germaine remained infirm. When she was again able to go out, she could be seen walking around the village with her lame foot, hobbling in an awkward fashion. It was pitiful to see the happy little girl of yesterday become so crippled and deformed. She had begun to carry her cross, as she felt constant torment in her body. Her leg remained painful; when a wound formed, nothing was able to cure it.

But already the mystery was at work, and the grace of election was bringing about its first fruits. Far better than any maternal exhortations, infirmity broke the violence of a temperament which could have become dangerous. A change took place in the little one: she seemed more serious, more patient, more detached from her impulsive will. It was as though the lancet had struck that which was most marked in her, her energy: not to defeat it, but to better it, to discipline and elevate it to a more lofty plane.

Her natural energy changed its orientation: rather than being impulsive, her spirit would turn inward to grow in depth. Her power of affection and her great sensitivity would become focused on these two objects of her love: God and her family.

Piety permeated her life. One of her great occupations was to pick flowers with which she would adorn the altars or, at home, the statue of the Blessed Mother. One could frequently find her in the church—she had only to cross her yard to get there—where she could be seen praying with a mental repose surprising for one of her age.

The second pole of Germaine's life was her family. She had an ardent family spirit, even more so now that her infirmity kept her inside more.

Also, among these simple people, attached to traditions, life was centered strongly around the home. No one ever got bored around the house: all gathered together in the family room and had fun among themselves, proving that they did not need exterior distractions. On Sundays, some relatives would be invited over; the father, who was lively and a brilliant talker, excelled at entertaining company. The mother was rather quiet but never stopped inventing games. A pleasant happiness reigned in the family of Germain Castang.

But then, around this time, the atmosphere began changing little by little. In spite of his courage, Germain suffered some reversals of fortune.

Little Maine could not yet understand what was happening, but she watched those dear faces become bitter. Her father lost his good humor and became difficult and impatient, and the child sometimes saw tears in her mother's eyes.

In spite of her lame foot, Little Maine sometimes followed her brothers and sisters on some short walk. One day they returned all proud of themselves, carrying with them a provision of magnificent chestnuts which, without any evil intentions, they had happily plundered. They were received in a fitting manner. "You little thieves!" cried Madame Castang, "have you no shame? Go take those back to their owner and beg his pardon on your knees." The sheepish band executed her orders and learned a lesson in how honesty was understood by the Castangs.

Germaine had lost nothing of her decisive spirit, and her courage remained intact. Whether it was a question of provoking a nest of hornets or surmounting some obstacle, she was always among the first to lead in the undertaking. She had a daring little way of greeting anyone, no matter whom, by looking them straight in the eye—which made her mother say: "That girl has enough nerve to make six horsemen dismount!"

That was not too serious, but there came a time that her strong will showed itself more dangerously. In the course of a dispute with an older brother, her bad leg put her in a position of inferiority. Therefore Germaine ventured to take down her father's rifle and, thus armed, pursued the "enemy"—who was fleeing, driven on by terrifying shrieks. This time the punishment was exemplary: besides the correction at home, her mother took her to school the next day and, in front of the whole class, related the crime and revealed the culprit. Beneath the reproaches of both mother and school mistress, Germaine took the humiliation amid sobs.

Madame Castang, who cherished her little Maine doubly because of her great suffering, had no intention of making a spoiled child of her.

A "Little Saint"

Germaine had not reached 10 years before she became nicknamed "the little saint." Her big faults, it seems, had disappeared. There were no more fits of temper; rather, a remarkable equilibrium was established in this young soul. Her great energy, which remained the predominant characteristic of her temperament, was turned entirely to practicing virtue: a perfect submission, a totally unexpected patience in such an imp, a self-mastery which reproached—and at the price of what efforts! She checked the movements of her bubbling vivacity. It was said that she was graced with the most pleasing natural gifts in the world; but in her eyes, it was the strong Castang will that burned inside her.

Germaine was charmingly serious and reasonable for her age, already reflecting the uprightness of her mother so well that, even then, she had acquired among the family members a veritable authority. She was loved for her good character and for her constant good humor amidst pains that never left her. This persistent gaiety was her victory over the trial: she had accepted this "good suffering," she was won over, and she began to love it.

A small event reveals Germaine's care not to defend herself from her cross and shows what degree of self control she had reached. The Castangs had a neighbor who grew strawberries, and Germaine was authorized to take her little brothers for walks on his land. Now, it happened one day that the precious strawberries were stolen. Convinced that Germaine was the cause of the pilfering, the owner came, fuming with rage, to complain to Madame Castang. Germaine's mother could not believe her ears. "What?" she asked, "it was you who did this?" But the furious man went on: "Eh! do you think she'll own up? If a rat's tail came out of her mouth, she would still deny it!" Germaine became pale: to hear herself treated as a thief and a liar—she who never told a lie, who was uprightness and delicacy itself! Indignation made her blood boil.

But that lasted only a moment; suppressing her emotion, she lowered her head and accepted the humiliation. She had learned to rise above self-love; already her life was elsewhere.

It was at this time (1886) that the old Church of Saint-Loup was demolished, to be replaced by the present Gothic structure dedicated to Sainte Quitterie. During the construction, Germaine's uncle, Etienne Castang, put a small tobacco-drying building that he owned at the disposal of the pastor for worship. It was very near his brother's, and the building was very rustic. Germaine did her best to decorate the building by bringing a profusion of flowers for the improvised altar.

She would often lead her little brothers and sisters there, and, like an experienced teacher, would speak to them of Jesus and of the Blessed Virgin Mary, making them pray with her. The Pastor, Abbé Theillet, looked upon these visits with amusement. On any other occasion he might have frowned upon the intrusion of this band of urchins into his church, but if Germaine was there he knew he could be at peace; she was an advantageous substitute as catechist.

Another place where Germaine was at home was the school. This modest village school was run, at that time, by religious of St. Joseph of Aubenas. The teaching was excellent, but the Sisters were even more devoted to the forming of souls.

Germaine found there the same spirit as in her family, the same spiritual atmosphere, the same lofty, entirely supernatural view of life. There was an assured consistency in her education. The religious Sisters were, for Madame Castang, the best auxiliaries of her maternal guidance. There, too, the child heard God spoken of, as well as the importance of responsibility, the goodness of suffering, and Heaven. She loved the good Sisters. One word was enough to make her obey immediately.

At school there was great devotion to the "Good St. Anne." One day, a young Sister came to replace the sick Mistress. Germaine, who was still very small, did not find her to her liking. "I want to stay with *you*," she said to the superior. "Then you want to make St. Anne cry?" she was asked. "Oh, no!" the child replied and went submissively to her place. The next day, she went spontaneously to her place and said: "Today I will not make St. Anne cry, I will make her laugh!"

On Thursdays, Germaine would spend the entire day at school. She felt quite at home with the Sisters. They, too, liked to have little Maine among them, for her presence was a grace.

It was thus that her soul opened to the attraction of the religious life at so young an age. In those childhood years her vocation awakened in her, as happens in pure and simple hearts. She spoke of it to her teachers. When her older sister Lucie left the family to take the veil among the religious of Aubenas, it was with envy that Germaine saw her leave. She was yet to pass through many hardships before being able to realize her dreams.

The lessons in charity she received from her parents made such a profound impression that she extended charity to all creatures; a witness worthy of the seraphic St. Francis of Assisi. Some swallows, taking advantage of a broken window pane, were allowed to install their nest in an unoccupied room of the house, and every year the winged tenants returned to take up lodging in the inviting abode, which they sometimes filled with their chirping.

Madame Castang always had a few clients, sick persons or poor beggars, upon whom to lavish her goodness, and Germaine participated in this charity. They had a neighbor named Cadette who was ill and very unhappy. The little one went to visit her every morning, rendering her all sorts of services and having a wonderful understanding of how to cheer her up. It seemed that her greatest happiness was to do good.

At home, Germaine's whole life was summed up in this: self-sacrifice, thinking only of others. The pet child had become the big sister who took care of the younger ones: Benjamin, Judith (also called Lubine) and Lucia, who was born after the death of little Lucien. More than a big sister, one could say she was for them like a little mother. She put them to bed, she bathed them, and she filled in for her mother in whatever way she could.

Little Maine's heart would break to see how her poor mother's work increased. She would start her chores as soon as she returned from school. For Germaine there was no time for play.

It was impressive to see this sickly child, having already grown up and having matured through suffering and love, giving herself in sacrifice for her family.

Griefs

The Castangs had a considerable estate, and it seems that the family was, at that time, one of the most notable in the town. Germain had shared well in the inheritance, and if he had had the good sense of his brother Etienne, he, together with his large family, would have lived in an enviable abundance. But his ambition lost him everything.

He was intelligent and resourceful, energetic and very active, even fearless; but he had equally marked faults. He was too impulsive and enterprising a character, he was imprudent, knowing neither how to foresee nor calculate. He tried everything, leaving one endeavor for another, persevering in nothing and so encountering only failure at every turn.

The house he built was far too large, and the family occupied only a part of it. It was never finished, and still today some interior walls are missing. The cafe and grocery store he opened on their ground level never did yield a profit. He soon left to his wife the troubles of commerce and tried cultivating a piece of land near the Bournegue, digging a reservoir and installing an irrigation system. But he neglected his crops and got the idea into his head to find a remedy against phylloxera. He invented one, the sale of which could have been quite lucrative if his demands had not been so exorbitant: he asked the State for no less than 2 million francs! The affair remained without an outcome. Amid all these occupations, he conducted on all sides the most diverse businesses—in which he never persevered.

All this devoured his income and yielded nothing in return. Germain took out some loans, and the debts accumulated. The family's situation became alarming. His affable character had gained for him the confidence of many, and some easy money—but when the money lenders saw his enterprises failing one after the other, they became fearful. They began to pressure him, and instead of using diplomacy, he got angry, alienating his creditors and thoroughly ruining his career. He ended up finding himself with his back to the wall.

The poor man became bitter, capricious and irascible. In the village he was avoided, and people gossiped about him, calling him "Bluster." At home he showed a detestable ill-humor, criticizing everybody and becoming angry at little nothings. The oldest sons, who were big boys now and worked on nearby farms, rebelled against their father's caprices and reproached him for squandering the money that they had earned for the family. These were painful scenes, often violent, which poisoned the once so cordial atmosphere of the home.

These were not bad boys. Louis was mild and peaceful. Levy showed a natural earnestness but seemed, as well as Guilbert, to be of a less easy-going temperament. Above all, it was the harshness with which their father continued to treat Madame Castang that made them rise up against him. The saintly woman endured it all, and though the suffering made her shed copious tears, she never once complained. It was her poor husband whom she pitied, and she responded to his brutality and irritation with only more gentleness. But the children remained indignant.

Germaine had far too much respect and affection for her father to allow herself to make any observations. Being too humble to take sides, she suffered in silence these quarrels which pitted against each other those whom she loved and honored more than anyone else in the world. It was a cruel pain to see the peace and serenity of the family degraded and ruined before her very eyes, and her heart broke to see her mother cry. Amidst these sorrows, anxieties and sometimes even violence, Germaine continued on in her apprenticeship in suffering.

In 1887, the family found itself in an alarming state of extreme poverty. They barely had enough to eat;

these people who had themselves shown such charity toward others were reduced to asking for help.

Germaine had brought gifts to her teachers when the Castangs were the benefactors of the Sisters, but now the roles were reversed. It was the Sisters who gave bread and whatever they could to aid her unfortunate parents. And one day, the misfortune they had feared fell upon the family. Being fed up, the creditors came after Germain Castang; his land, home, furniture and all his possessions were sold.

The Tragic Years

The blow was terrible. Neither roof, nor resources—nothing. It was complete misery. What was to become of them?

In the course of his multiple enterprises, Germain Castang had connected with a relative who, at his death, had left to Germain a meadow within the parish of Labouquerie, about four kilometers from Nojals. For whatever reason, this property escaped confiscation. Seeing that he was on the brink of catastrophe, Germain had hastily built a shelter on this property; it was there, for lack of anything better, he decided to house his family.

And so they left Nojals. For little Maine, it was the ruin of her young life, the sacrifice of all that she had held dear: her paternal home so full of memories, which was now being lived in by others; her dear church where she loved to pray; her friends, her relatives, the good Sisters . . . More than that, Germaine's dream was moved further from realization; her First Holy Communion would be put off and until when? What a heartbreak! She was only ten, and that is quite young to experience such misery.

But what pierced her heart above all was the family's desolation. Poor parents! To have suffered so many pains, worked so hard, spent themselves so devotedly only to arrive at this: total ruin and flight to hide their distress and their shame. To be driven from the hearth which was the fruit of their patience and love! My God! Only to go where?

The "Castang meadow," as it is still called today, is situated in the middle of the forest, at the entrance into the highland. It is not easy to find. From the road to Monpazier, one takes the forest path that leads to Sainte-Croix. Having passed the hamlet of Salabert, comprised of two houses, one takes a right turn through the fields, and through a clearing in the underbrush, one stumbles upon the meadow. The land is a vast sloping terrain, encircled by the forest on all sides and completely isolated. At the height of the prairie, Germain had built his hut with improvised materials.

One day before dawn, in order not to be seen, the poor exiles set out on their way with heavy hearts, taking nothing with them but some worn clothes loaded on a donkey cart. Among the sad spoils wrested from the disaster, the sole object of value was a beautiful crucifix which Germain himself had bought and from which he did not wish to be separated. In her arms Madame Castang carried little Lucia, who was but one year old.

After a long walk in half-darkness, the caravan entered the humid meadow at dusk. What dismay these unfortunate people experienced at the sight of their new lodging: four low walls of rough masonry, a roof of tiles placed—for better or for worse—on top of a lattice of poles that was sustained on the inside by poorly squared props, a door through which one could pass only by ducking and, at the top of one of the walls, a single opening, which served as the only window. The interior of the shelter was two meters fifty by seven meters (about 8 feet x 21 feet), and one could just barely stand up in it. There was not a shadow of furniture. The floor was the bare ground, and in place of a chimney there was a hole in the roof. Today, one can still see the traces of soot all along the wall under this hole.

The Castangs found themselves in a sinister solitude, deprived of any view but the forest on all sides, without any communication and far from any inhabited place, with the exception of the two little houses of Salabert some few hundred meters away.

They settled within the hovel as well as they could, camping out provisionally. But, alas, this "waiting" was to end up lasting a long time—three fatal years.

A country woman who knew the Castangs during this period described the miserable household thus: At one end the donkey was tethered, one cow was housed in a shed adjoining the hut, and the family occupied the rest of the shelter. There were no chairs, only logs on which to sit. Everyone lay down at night on a sort of common camp mat; toward the middle of the structure, against the wall, was a wood fire which, lacking a chimney, filled the place with pungent smoke, making the air, already foul from the donkey's odor, dim and unhealthy.

Madame Castang made some large corn crepes, and these, together with some milk and the turnips or potatoes which they were permitted to grow in a neighbor's field, constituted the essentials of the daily menu. They drew water at the edge of the property, where a thin muddy trickle oozed up from the ground.

Mr. Castang did not help the family except in bouts. He was almost always away in search of work, but he stubbornly continued to seek his utopian solutions, which never did materialize.

In the summer, when the older children found a bit of work on farms, they brought back some resources which made life tolerable, though the heat rendered the cramped shelter uninhabitable. On the other hand, the winter was atrocious. Nothing came in then; it was a situation of dire want. The family suffered from hunger and cold. Trapped within the deserted fields, without so much as a path for access, the family huddled around the fire. The fire gave out smoke but did not heat the room, which was open to the cold air of the countless drafts which filtered through the joints of the building and the cracks in the tiles. This was an infested atmosphere, without any distraction but the noise of strong gusts of wind in the forest and the cries of nocturnal animals.

The Castang family were far from their fine home in Nojals and from the comfortable family room where little Maine had loved to keep house with her mother, who had delighted in tidying up and entertaining guests. How could one keep house in this crowded hovel which was always covered with charcoal dust and dirt from the fields? And whom could they possibly entertain? Everything was darkened by the smoke, and dishes and utensils were almost non-existent.

Germaine, however, devoted herself to making their sojourn there as little hideous as possible; sweeping, cleaning, arranging wildflowers in a pot in front of the crucifix, shaking out the covers, mending threadbare garments, seeing to the donkey and looking after the

children: she was "as good as always" at everything
that she ever did.

Meanwhile, her illness grew worse. She limped more
and more, and her foot had turned under completely.
She walked on her ankle, which was painfully crushed,
and the wound on her leg became grotesque. Her father
was occasionally heard to say: "It is going to rain
because worms are coming out of Germaine's leg." It
was ghastly. The poor child needed care urgently, but
no care was possible in that forsaken place.

She heroically hid her torture so that she might not
add to the family's pain. It was Germaine, the crippled
and suffering one, who brought a ray of sunshine into
the usual distress. She always succeeded, even in the
most somber hours, in creating a joy and energy which
sustained, encouraged and comforted her family, and
she did not cease to sacrifice herself for others.

Lucie, the religious, was her confidant (by corre-
spondence). During this period, Louis, the oldest, left
for his military service. He was Germaine's favorite
brother, the one who understood her best. "Like Germaine," wrote Lucie, "he was a living copy of his mother:
the same energy, the same mildness of character, the
same faith, the same piety, the same good sense, the
same spirit of order and good management, the same
love for work and devotion to the family." Germaine
was happy to see him leave this sad place, but for her
it was a painful privation, and the family lost his precious help. But she remained to the end, comforting
the others without ever receiving any comfort in return.

Madame Castang showed herself to be worthy of such
a daughter. Tormented by a painful hernia, she too suffered in body as well as in soul. No more than Germaine did she speak of her ills. She faced her trials

with an invincible faith and an admirable strength of soul.

In the midst of this misery, she gave birth to two more sons: Paul and Edmond. One can imagine the additional worry that these sad births caused her.

Moreover, Madame Castang found the means to take in another child too. Madame L____ of Nojals had a two-month-old baby which she was watching waste away, for she could not nurse the poor child herself. She urgently sought a wet nurse, and Madame Castang came to mind. Unfortunately, the two families were not on good terms, undoubtedly following Germain's dealings, and so Madame Castang was disregarded. What then should she do? Overcome by maternal love, Madame L____ arrived one day at the shelter on the Castang meadow carrying her infant in her arms.

It was a daring step. Madame Castang was herself nursing a child. And this little one that Madame L____ was bringing to her was sickly, covered with scabs and hideous and repulsive to behold. But that is precisely what touched the heart of this generous woman. Forgetting past misunderstandings and overcoming her disgust, Marie Castang took the child to nurse it. She saved his life, and he became a strong and healthy man.

However, in the long run the Castangs' situation became tragic. The family's health weakened, along with their morale. There was nothing on the horizon for them to look forward to. The months, the years passed without bringing them a ray of hope. How long would this misery last, this inhuman existence in this filthy den? The little ones were wasting away from hunger.

Germaine deprived herself for their sake. She pretended not to be hungry so that they might have a little more to eat, but she was cruelly tortured by star-vation. She was getting thinner and thinner under their very eyes. On one occasion she accompanied her mother, together with a younger brother, to a tinsmith's in Labouquerie. His heart was pierced at seeing their lit-tle hollow and emaciated faces. Having pity on them, he had them sit down and gave them food to eat.

One day, Germaine could hold out no longer. There was nothing left in the shelter, the children were cry-ing, her mother was tormented. Gathering her courage, she took the wheelbarrow, and for some hours, limping and stumbling under the heavy weight, she made the rounds of the nearby farms, begging alms. The proud Germaine Castang made a beggar of herself for love of her family. She returned exhausted, overwhelmed with pain, but she brought them food.

She could not often repeat such a deed: it would have killed her. What could the family do? They were in their third winter in this hovel, and they began to despair of ever getting through it. But their "morning" was about to dawn:

One day, their father returned full of joy, for he had found work: nothing brilliant, but the income would be sufficient to support the family. He had rented a little house in the town of Saint-Genes. They were to leave this "hell"—at last!—to go live in the city.

The Hospital

Bordeaux, it was an exile again, and even more than before. They left not only their village, but also their native region. They were uprooted and at a loss amid the anonymity of the city suburbs.

But everything was a blessing after the nightmare

they had lived through. They could begin again to be alive, in a house and among mankind. The children would have something to eat and would go to school. The family arrived in the city around the spring of 1890.

Louis was still in the army, and Lucie was in the convent of the Sisters of St. Joseph of Privas, under the name of Sr. Saint Germain. Two children had died, but there remained eight children with the Castang parents. Guilbert, the oldest at home, was 16, and Edmond, the youngest, was still a babe-in-arms.

The new dwelling was at number 37 of the rue Puysegur, a narrow street with low houses on the outskirts of the city. Theirs was a single story house, of puny appearance, but it offered enough space to house the numerous family.

Germain Castang was employed as a grocer's aide, and he delivered bread. His income was just sufficient to feed the family. This was no longer misery, only poverty.

Germaine wanted to return to school without delay to resume studying her catechism: she was entering her 13th year! But once again she renounced her desires and, for the first few months, remained at home to help her mother.

There was much to do in setting up the new household. Almost everything was lacking since misfortune had struck their home. They acquired some worn-out old furniture, bought second-hand, and there was no end to the cleaning needed to give the poor little house at least a decent appearance. Then there were the children: Germaine had become their active and devoted little mother.

It was high time to look after Germaine's bad leg.

Madame Castang herself needed care, but for the moment neither the one nor the other had any time. Besides, how could they afford to pay a doctor? But Divine Providence could.

In the beginning of 1891, Germaine's arm was bitten by a dog. For fear of rabies, she was sent to a nearby hospital. The doctors naturally examined her leg as well. "My child," they said, "this needs attention, and without delay. Go ask your mother if you can be admitted to the hospital, and we will make you well."

On February 7, 1891, she was admitted to the Children's Hospital on the road to Bayonne. The establishment, then newly founded, was a handsome and vast modern hospital, of a radiant appearance, with its extensive lawns and flower beds; its numerous pavilions, long halls and bright single rooms. It was worthy of the Sisters of St. Vincent de Paul, who are rightly called: Daughters of Charity.

Germaine's paralyzed left foot was operated on, and the surgery was a complete success. The foot was made straight, and Germaine was able to walk more easily and with much less of a limp. While she was recovering, her leg was in a cast and she was looked after with special care, for she attracted the affection of all. Now it was her turn to be petted and surrounded by maternal affection. Her heart overflowed with gratitude.

When Germaine could walk again, her spirit of self-sacrifice was as strong as ever, and she wanted to make herself useful. To show her gratitude, she asked to be allowed to help the other children in the ward. Good Sr. Adelaide was unable to refuse her. So, there was the little infirmarian going from one bed to another, assisting the religious in making the rounds and entertaining the sick little ones. Germaine was excellent at bringing a smile to a face in tears. She also spoke to the children of the Good God and taught them to pray. Sr. Adelaide, who had known the Castang family, spoke of Germaine in these terms: "She was very brave, and she had such wisdom, good sense, delicacy and patience—far above others her age. She was the living copy of the heart and virtues of her mother, whom I have always considered to be a very saintly woman."

Germaine was at home in this nice hospital, surrounded by the care and affection of the good Sisters draped in their blue habits. She was healing and now life seemed to smile upon her. But it was not in God's plan that she linger in joy.

On February 28, little Edmond, the last born, was taken to the hospital afflicted with pneumonia. This poor child was also tubercular, and on May 4, he died at the age of one. A few days later an epidemic of measles raged within the family. Germaine watched her two little brothers and two little sisters admitted to the hospital one by one. The little girls recovered, but the boys both suffered complications and succumbed, one month apart. The parents' pain was heartrending.

It was in the face of this new sadness that, on July 30, Germaine returned to her family, where death's blow had been so cruel. Her heart broke at seeing the empty places.

However, her suffering in the family was not over.

Louis, the "good Louis," had returned from the army in an alarming state, no doubt "sent home because of illness." Having slept on the damp ground in the course of a maneuver, he had caught bronchitis, which had progressed dangerously. Now it was consumption (tuberculosis), and he was mortally ill. The family were to prepare for a new sorrow, the most devastating of all.

For Germaine this was a new reason to remain at home, and she did so with all her heart. But her mother was concerned for her future. Through the good offices of a priest, the Abbè Deym, Germaine was received as a boarder at a nearby establishment, "The Refuge of Nazareth," which took in poor and abandoned girls.

Shortly before her departure, a small incident opened Germaine's eyes to the dangers of the world and helped to detach her from it. One summer evening, her father took her to a festival in a neighboring suburb. She had become a very attractive girl, with a singularly expressive face. She was chatting with a group of friends and watching the fireworks in front of the church when a man, who had joined the company, began conversing with her and drawing her little by little away from her father, whom she thought was behind her. She suddenly realized her mistake and desired to return to the group, but the lurid individual held her and offered her some money if she would follow him.

Germaine understood that this man had evil intentions, and, taken by a terrible fright, she broke loose and fled with all her strength. She reached her father, trembling like a little bird escaped from a snare.

⤜ Chapter 2 ⤛

The Orphanage

The Refuge of Nazareth

THE REFUGE (also called the "Solitude") of Nazareth is located at the very end of the rue Saint-Genes, on the corner where it intersects with the Cours de l'Argonne and forms the Square of Saint-Genes. The establishment has a modern look, but it is a very old building. It was founded by the Sisters of Mary Joseph, who are also known as prison "specialists." It is they who served Saint Lazare in Paris and all the main prisons in France, with all the wisdom and devotion required of that delicate mission.

The "Solitude" included a penitentiary, an orphanage and a workshop. This division was apparent from the layout of the chapel. The nave was reserved for the public; in front of the Sister's pews were the orphans on the right and the boarders of the workshop on the left; and on either side of the choir there were two side chapels, hidden from view, which were reserved for the women prisoners.

It was to the workrooms that Germaine Castang was assigned when she entered Nazareth on September 12, 1891. This was another disappointment. She had been

looking forward to going to the school at the orphanage, for she wanted to continue her education. But seeing that they had set her up in the workroom, that
was fine, she would go to the workroom; she said not
a word, nor did she express any desire. She accepted
all with equal detachment, to her it was all good.
Besides, she would now learn her catechism, and that
was the important thing.

They began by giving her yet another name! Since
there was already another boarder by the name of
"Germaine," at Nazareth she would be called "Lucia."
This further accentuated the break with her past and,
in some ways, even with herself, but still she remained
quite indifferent. The only detail that was truly painful
to her was that, on account of her slight limp, she was
made to sit in one of the side chapels instead of being
placed in the nave with her companions from the workroom.

In order to initiate her into her work, Germaine was
adjoined with another border, a girl of very difficult
and rude character. At the least mistake of her apprentice, this monitor would become impatient and irate,
scolding her violently, chasing after her and bullying
her without pity. The little apprentice took all this
without complaint; only occasionally would a tear
escape her, but then she would set courageously back
to work, trying to understand and do better.

So revolting were the antics of this irascible monitor that the other students, full of compassion for the
"new one," counselled her to complain to the Mistress.
But Germaine invariably responded with her pleasant
smile: "Oh, no! If she scolds me, it is for my own good.
I should be corrected if I want to learn to work. I offer
it to the Good Lord, and I'll be happy for it later."

Germaine also had other points on which to practice resignation. Her great sorrow was to be so far from her loved ones. She felt so alone in this place, still so unfamiliar! Now, Mr. Castang delivered the bread to the institution. One day when the students were in the dining room, he was seen next door. Germaine was permitted to go say hello to him. What joy! To see her dear Papa! She approached full of delight, but at the moment she was about to hug him she was called back rudely: "Get back in there with your companions!"

More than once Germaine was punished unjustly, but she always accepted the punishment without saying one word in self-defense.

Germaine's constant serenity was the fruit of a sometimes very fierce interior battle, for her extreme vivacity was still far from being dead. One of her companions, Jeanne Bégué—called Joanès at the boarding school—who soon became Germaine's great friend, confirmed this with some anecdotes from their early years together:

"One day, by mistake Germaine was poured a very bitter glass of quinine instead of wine. She simply swallowed it without flinching.

"The extent of her self-mastery and detachment was not difficult to discover; one need only see her in the chapel.

"She was the life and soul of recreation, but at the first sound of the bell she immediately cut short her play and resumed her recollection.

"She was available for any service, ready for any sacrifice. She could be asked to do anything. Whenever anyone needed anything, it was to her that they went: 'Oh, Lucia, could you do me a favor? Could you mend this? Could you trim this?' 'Yes, let me have it,' she would respond. 'Lucia, you wouldn't have a needle to lend me?' 'Yes, here it is.' 'Lucia, I lost my thimble.' 'Oh, here is mine.' Never did she refuse to strip herself for the sake of others."

"At the Refuge there was a frail old woman, 'the poor Mémé Joseph,' whom Germaine had taken under her wing. She was diligent in her work, yet still found time to care for her. The old woman was abusive by her own will, and she would shout from the other end of the hall: 'Mémé Joseph is calling you!' And every time, Germaine would run to her, always with the same haste."

The other boarders would sometimes amuse themselves by asking Germaine for some fictitious service to "get her going." An "Oh!" with a smile was her only reaction. She had a charming gracefulness in entertaining others at her own expense. Joanès remembered the powdered crepes made with pepper which she had prepared as a joke for the carnival and which Germaine had swallowed without wincing, for the greater pleasure of others!

The Most Beautiful Day

In the meantime, the day was approaching on which would be fulfilled one of the greatest dreams of Germaine's life: she was finally to be admitted to the holy Table of Our Lord. It was this day that she had aspired to since her childhood, and now she was almost 15. Her greatest privation during the somber years in the shelter of Salabert had been being far from the church.

At the Refuge it was the custom every Sunday to read aloud the notes of the previous week, and then, once a month, there followed the granting of rewards. The proclamation was made before the Superior—and was listened to, as one can imagine, in religious silence. On one Sunday, the notes on Germaine had been particularly laudatory; there, in the middle of the impressive silence that followed the reading, she rose and addressed the Superior: "Dear Mother, in recompense, allow me to leave the side chapel and to sit before the tabernacle. From where I am, I cannot see Him, Jesus!" The Superior, who was moved by the fervor that prompted this ingenuous request, could not but comply. It was a wonderful day for Germaine. Even though her infirmity threw off the line a little, it was a benefit for all to see the "little violet" praying before the Blessed Sacrament.

Because of Germaine's great desire, her piety and her virtues, the Superior made a unique exception for her, admitting her to the sodality of the "Children of Mary" even before her First Communion. Her First Communion was set for June 16, 1892, the Feast of Corpus Christi.

In the course of the preparatory retreat, Germaine was called upon to have the appearance of her leg assessed. "Oh no!" she cried in distress, "I cannot go; this is my retreat, I do not want to speak!" She was told: "It is your duty because you are being told to go." Immediately she smiled, stood up and went to the parlor with her usual promptness.

On the morning of that beautiful day, when Germaine put on her white dress (the great source of distraction for the little daughters of Eve), she seemed to pay hardly any attention to it.

After the ceremony, someone having called her, Germaine started to run. But her mother was present; she had attended the Mass with the two little sisters. "Germaine," she said, "do not forget that you have Jesus in your heart." "Oh! Yes," Germaine replied, "I must not run." "You will see," whispered Madame Castang, "that I will have a second daughter a religious."

Germaine's father, who was no doubt detained by his work, was not able to attend the ceremony, but he joined the family later in the day. When embracing Germaine that evening he said, "My daughter, I am pleased and proud of you: you were the most serious and recollected of all."

Shortly after her First Communion, Germaine received Confirmation in the Cathedral of Bordeaux. The bishop gave her the name "Clare." Was this a presage of things to come?

A Devastated Home

On the day of her First Communion, the great grace which Germaine asked of Our Lord was to become a religious.

She opened herself to her confessor, Fr. Campan, who was a saintly man. But the old priest had some different ideas. "You will enter at 21," he told her, "or, if you want to go before that, you will spend a year in the world." That was his usual method.

But here the will of Germaine Castang regained her rights. Wait another seven years? Ah, no! She spoke to the Superior, Mother Marie Saint-Pierre, who had known how to appreciate Germaine and would have been quite happy to accept her. The Superior sent Germaine's application to the motherhouse of Dorat. The answer was a flat refusal: the infirmity of the aspirant placed an obstacle to her admission.

It was a hard blow for Germaine, because it affected her future: where would she be accepted if she was refused here? Again, the beautiful dream was far off, and more remote than ever. Her hope was feeble, almost extinct.

No doubt Germaine would have gone to knock on other doors if she had had the time. But she was already faced with new trials.

One day in the year 1892, her mother came to announce some big news: The family was to leave Bordeaux! Her father was to be employed as domestic help by the Marquise de Lascaze at the castle of Montauban, where Madame Castang would also be employed. It would be new uprooting! Germaine would no longer even have the joy of her parents' visits to the Refuge. The castle was located in Casseuil, which was 60 kilometers from Bordeaux in the region of La Reole. The rest of the family moved, and Germaine alone was left in the "Solitude" of Nazareth.

With a heavy heart Germaine sunk into this new isolation, with nothing more than the mere memory of her family, and with sad thoughts of her poor, suffering mother reduced to servitude among strangers.

But this was only a prelude to the unhappiness that awaited her. On the morning of December 30 a religious took Germaine aside and, with an overwhelmed look, said to her: "My child, I have very sorrowful news to give you." "Oh!" cried the girl, "is it my brother Louis? Has he died?" "No, it is not Louis, it's . . ." She dared not finish. "But, who then? Tell me!" ". . . Your mother." And the Sister held out to Germaine the telegram which she had not been able to bring herself to show her the evening before.

This time the blow was too great, and so ruthless!

Germaine burst into sobs. Her mother! Her good and holy mother, for whom she had such tender devotion, had departed so suddenly, without even saying goodbye or blessing her one last time! This was so entirely unexpected! What had happened to her?

Germaine was stunned by the pain. Her first action was to throw herself at the feet of the Blessed Virgin. Then she left for Casseuil. She went by boat up the River Garonne. In the course of the trip, a woman noticed this child who was crying. The woman inquired about her trouble and took Germaine under her maternal protection. The boat was running late and stopped for the night at St. Pierre d'Aurillac. The compassionate stranger persuaded Germaine to stay with her, and the following morning, she had her driven by car to Casseuil.

Germaine arrived too late: the body had already been removed. She ran to the church, where the funeral service was underway. There she stopped in her tracks, heartsick at the sight of the bier. She was signalled to come forward, and sobbing, she went and leaned her head against the coffin, the only farewell she was allowed.

After the funeral, Germaine was told everything. Madame Castang's hernia had unexpectedly worsened; the Marquise had sent her to Bordeaux to have surgery, but in descending from the train at the station of Caudrot, she suddenly felt that she was *in extremis*. "I am dying," she said. "It is finished." She asked for a picture of Our Lady of Perpetual Help, and while praying to the Blessed Virgin, she died all alone, this valiant mother of 12 children. She was only 41 years old.

At the house a new grief awaited Germaine. Wasted by consumption, Louis was seriously ill. "Ah, here you are, my poor Germaine!" he murmured from his bed, extending an emaciated hand. Then they cried together, for they had nothing more to say to one another.

Broken down by sorrow, Mr. Castang could not function. Who would take care of this poor man? And the little ones? Lubine and Lucia were still with him, but at ages seven and six they still needed a mother, and Louis was in need of constant care. Germaine saw her duty clearly: "I will stay," she said; "I will replace my mother." She decided to leave the Refuge of Nazareth to resume her role as little mother—only this time, alongside her poor father.

The house was small and there was no bed for Germaine; but what did it matter? She lay a blanket on the floor, and that would suffice for sleeping, even though it was the middle of winter. In reality she did not sleep at all. Always alert to the needs of her beloved patient who required continual care, she spent most of the night at his side.

During the day she would keep house, look after her little sisters and comfort her father; and then, returning to Louis' bedside, she would care for his soul as well as his body. The pious young man was ready, accepting his fate with an admirable spirit of faith and desiring nothing more than to rejoin his mother in Heaven. He understood well when his saintly little sister spoke to him of the joy of seeing God, and he could not have found a sweeter angel to take him by the hand during his final passage.

Germaine set to work with complete self-forgetfulness. She could not last long at this rate. But had she ever measured her sacrifices? Was she going to do so now—now that she could see her family in such dire affliction and with so great a need?

In fact, it turned out that these days and nights of overwork would not last much longer. On the evening of January 6 the invalid let out a cry. Germaine and her father, who were in the next room, rushed in to see torrents of blood issuing from Louis' mouth, covering the bed and floor. It was the end. Germaine pointed to Heaven. Exhausted, Louis let his head drop and gently expired in her arms.

This last sorrow elucidated the unfortunate household of Germain Castang: his wife and six children, exactly half the family, had been taken from him through death; the older sons were on their own; the two daughters were taken care of: one being a religious and the other in boarding school; only he and the two little ones remained. On top of everything, he would have to leave the castle, for he could no longer perform the services all alone. He decided to liquidate the household: Lubine and Lucia would go to Nazareth with Germaine, and he would fend for himself.

And so it was with her two little sisters that Germaine returned to the Refuge at the beginning of 1893. The good Superior had immediately agreed to receive Lubine and Lucia, and she welcomed the three girls with open arms.

Shortly after Germaine's return, yet another source of suffering was discovered. Being pressed by questions, she finally admitted that her leg was in pain. Joanès wanted to examine it, and saw with horror the large open wound on Germaine's ankle. It was very painful to have removed the folds in the stockings, which lodged in the wound and stuck to it with encrusted blood. "Why didn't you take care of this sooner?" Joanès cried. "Oh," Germaine responded simply, "I had so much to do at home that I didn't think of it."

Solitude

The three years that followed were years of darkness. Germaine, become "Lucia" again, brought back with her from Casseuil another sorrow to add to the others. She was unable to forget the spectacle of desolation which she had left behind, and the memory of her father was a permanent scar on her heart. Her letters to him during this period reveal this sorrowful compassion and her attempts to console him in his loneliness.

But not having any immediate duties toward her dispersed family, Germaine's thoughts began turning in another direction: perhaps she could once again take up the plan so dear to her—to become a religious. But this time she felt apprehension; the previous failure had diminished her hope.

She asked herself, "If God wants me to be a religious, why does He not take away my infirmity, if that is the obstacle?" In fact, that seemed to be quite logical, so she began to pray for the healing of her leg, something she had never done before. She even obtained permission to go along on a pilgrimage, resolving to beg Our Lady for this favor in Lourdes.

The pilgrimage was a feast for her piety, but her hope of being healed was disappointed.

Back at the Refuge, the boarders' long walks often took Germaine to the outskirts of the nearby town of Talence. There, just 15 minutes from the Refuge of Nazareth, was a Poor Clare convent, the Monastery of the Ave Maria. Today the surroundings have been developed into domestic suburbs, but at that time the monastery was still out in the country.

In the course of the summer of 1893, Germaine spoke

with Fr. Firmin, the Guardian of the Franciscan friary which was next door to the Refuge, entreating him to be her advocate with the Poor Clares. She anxiously awaited their response. Again, it was a refusal: they thought the candidate was too young; but even more, her physical state was a serious concern.

Germaine was heartbroken. They did not want her; not even in the cloister? She could not understand. Father explained to her that a monastery is not and cannot be a hospital. In order to fulfill one's vocation, it is indispensable that the observances be strictly kept and that dispensations be reduced to the minimum. Therefore, in the interest of all, an Order cannot accept those who, from the start, have need of such dispensations. Moreover, the Rule of the Poor Clares was so difficult that Germaine was not cut out physically to endure its rigors.

Was it all over then? Germaine could not give up. She wrote to her sister Lucie, who was now Sr. Marie de St. Germain of the Sisters of St. Joseph, and begged her to intercede with her Superiors that they might receive her there, for the Rule of the Sisters of St. Joseph was less rigorous, and she would be able to follow it. But, alas, Lucie responded that Germaine's health would be an insurmountable obstacle and begged her to resign herself.

One after the other, all the lights were dimmed and extinguished. Germaine would have to spend the rest of her days in this orphanage where she had happened to be thrown by her miserable fate, to do the sewing and to watch and entertain the children—for at the Refuge the Sisters were apt to look upon her as an assistant Mistress.

The Sisters of Nojals had once promised Madame

Castang that they would adopt the two youngest girls if death should surprise her before she had secured their future. They remembered their promise and claimed the children. It was decided that Lubine would go to Aubenas to be with her sister, Sr. Marie de St. Germain, and Lucia would go to the Sisters of Nojals. It seems that this arrangement did not last though, for a short time later we find both of the girls with Lucie in Aubenas.

At any rate, toward the end of September of 1893, the pastor of Nojals came to Nazareth to take the children to their destinations. Germaine accompanied them to the train station; nothing on her countenance betrayed her great pain.

Now that she was alone at the Refuge, the weight of abandonment fell like lead upon her shoulders. A wave of desolation engulfed her soul. Oh, now it was truly "Solitude!"

A time of real abnegation followed: news was rare and always sad. One time it was Guilbert, who had become ill and was admitted to the hospital; another time it was Levy, of whom her father complained. Neither of the two boys seemed to reach an understanding with Mr. Castang. Germaine knew almost nothing of what was going on with them. She repeatedly wrote letters to try to contact them, but in vain. After a while she no longer even knew where her father was. The letters she wrote did not reach him or remained unanswered. Germain Castang seems to have lived the life of a vagabond during this time, going from one place to another in search of business. And on top of it all, he too was ill and spoke of going to the hospital. Only once or twice did Mr. Castang come to see his daughter at the Refuge.

In her loneliness, Germaine's broken dream came back to her, flooding her soul; her desire to become a religious was stronger and more painful than ever. "My God!" she would pray, "make me a religious; and then, if it pleases You, make me suffer much—only do make me a religious! Oh yes, my God, make me die a religious!" If she could not be a Poor Clare, she would enter anywhere; it did not matter where. She persisted in begging her sister, Sr. Marie de St. Germain, who apparently was given some difficulty in her community on this subject and ended up not responding. The doors of solitude closed upon Germaine.

Final Trials

Germaine's charity naturally continued to extend to the members of her family. She envied Lucie for having the "dear little ones." She would mail nice maternal letters to them, and for the New Year she sent a package of gifts she had bought for them with the few *sous* she had earned at the Refuge. The rest of her purse was used to help Guilbert, who was ill. For herself she had need of nothing.

Germaine's great concern was the constant tension which existed between her two brothers and their father. But the brothers were not the only ones at fault. Mr. Castang had returned to Nojals all alone. Beaten by life and bitter, he withdrew into a tiny hovel, alienating himself from his family and speaking to no one except to complain or argue.

He refused to receive Levy. As for Guilbert, he had joined the army and had left for Madagascar without seeing his father. Germaine was grieved over this misunderstanding. Certainly, if she had been there, she could have arranged everything and restored peace among her loved ones. Finally, she could bear it no longer and asked to be allowed to visit them.

She made the trip to Nojals, where she revisited, not without some melancholy, the church, the school and her dear native home. Her father received her coldly. But could he resist the grace and profound affection of his little Maine for long, he who was no longer loved by anyone? Germaine disarmed him entirely.

She then hurried to La Reole, where Levy lived. He was far more difficult to persuade; he did not dare believe the miracle worked by his sister and dreaded standing before his father. But he too ended up giving in. Germaine went on ahead to Nojals to prepare the way with their father, then Levy presented himself. The two men shook hands, and in a joyful atmosphere of peace created by Germaine, the old wounds were soon healed. The day ended in a happiness that had been long forgotten.

Levy remained a week in Nojals, and he promised that he would return to live there. Germaine herself profited from her sojourn to Nojals and Saint-Avit-Senieur by seeing once again family members and old acquaintances. These visits, however, were not without the pain of being snubbed, for she was, after all, the daughter of Germain Castang, and village resentments are tenacious! Particularly at her Uncle Etienne's, she found bitterness. He himself was a good and peaceful man, but his wife had a sharp tongue and caused Germaine to "suffer cruelly."

One of Germaine's first visits was to the Sisters at the school. She recalled, "My good Teachers received me with open arms, and I threw myself into those same arms which had opened to me in times past." Another motive made this encounter of great value. Still determined to follow God's will, Germaine had not renounced the idea of becoming a religious, nor had she given up in her efforts. Neither the many refusals nor the discouraging responses of Lucie had managed to deter her resolute will. She seriously considered writing to the Superior General of Aubenas herself, and, naturally, she spoke about this to the Sisters of Nojals. But their response put those plans to an end.

It was from her father that she received the last wounds, and they were cruel ones. Seeing again his daughter, who was so sweet, so affectionate, and who took such pains to care for his smallest needs, Mr. Castang had begun to nurture hopes of creating a little home and keeping her with him. Germaine had been happy to return "home" and to be with her father, whom she loved so much—to show her devotion to him, to keep house and to be his "little Maine" as before. But could she commit herself without knowing if God was calling her or not? God had called, and in spite of the refusals, she felt it. The Master's words were there running through all her desires: "If anyone would come after Me, and does not prefer Me to his father, he cannot be My disciple."

Before making a decision, Germaine thought she should get some advice in order to clarify what her duty was. She asked Lucie. Lucie opposed her father's plans and encouraged Germaine to remain at Nazareth for the time being; there she could at least live on the margins of the religious life and could pursue other avenues.

All of this Germaine explained to her father in the letter she wrote to him upon her return to Nazareth. To this very affectionate letter he did not respond.

The Doors Opened

The first ray of hope was given to Germaine during a pilgrimage to the sanctuary of Our Lady of Talence.

It was Easter Monday, April 6, 1896, a day still resonating with the joys of Easter and full of the beauty of spring. On that day, God Himself took Germaine by the hand to lead her to her destination.

The boarders had left on one of their long walks, but because of her infirmity, Germaine had stayed behind in the workroom. An assistant Mistress invited her to go on a pilgrimage to the sanctuary of Our Lady of Talence, and the two set out.

At the sanctuary, they remained a long time in prayer at the feet of the Blessed Virgin, after which Germaine's companion, Claire said: "I have an idea! Let's pass by the Poor Clares to say hello to Sr. Marie Francesca" (who was an extern Sister they knew). And so they went.

At the monastery, as Germaine conversed with Sr. Marie Francesca, she suddenly cried out: "How happy these sisters must be! I will never have such happiness. Oh, if only I could enter!" It was a cry from the heart which had burst forth without any forethought.

It was this exclamation which would open the doors for Germaine. "Would you like to speak to the Reverend Mother and explain your situation to her?" she was asked. Germaine would never have dreamed of asking; she would never have dared to ask.

Her heart pounded as she was led to the parlor. The grille curtain was drawn, and Germaine beheld four smiling nuns. The smiles of the Poor Clares put her immediately at ease. The Sisters questioned her, and soon it was their turn to be deeply moved.

All four were inspired to receive Germaine. At the
end of the interview, Germaine made a gesture of charming simplicity: "My Reverend Mothers," she said, "I
have spoken to you about my leg, but now I really
ought to show you how I walk." "Very well," said the
Mother Abbess; "if you walk around the parlor three
times without halting, I will accept you right away!"
Germaine did so, and the Mother Abbess dismissed her
with these sweet words: "Pray and hope."

It was too good to be true! Germaine was overcome
with joy, and she rejoined her companion shedding
tears for sheer happiness. It was so unexpected!

At the Refuge on the following Wednesday, Germaine
was called by Mother Marie St. Pierre, who had a letter for her from the Mother Abbess of the Poor Clares
announcing that Germaine Castang had been accepted
by the Monastery of the Ave Maria and inviting the
postulant to present herself the following Sunday. "Ah,
well! My sly little thing," she said teasingly, "what did
you do down there?" Germaine was so overcome with
happiness that she could answer nothing. The good
Superior embraced her tenderly, happy to see her desire
finally granted, for she had as much love as veneration for the Poor Clares. Everyone at Nazareth con-
gratulated Germaine and rejoiced with her, though they
were sad to be losing her. Only the rigid Fr. Campan
thought it good to admonish her that her entry was
against his principles. But in the end, he too "admired
the designs of God on this soul"—though God's designs
differed somewhat from his own.

When she returned to the monastery the following
Sunday, Germaine saw the entire community behind
the grille. The Sisters visited a long time with the

soon-to-be postulant. Her entrance day was fixed, barring impediment, for June 12, the Feast of the Sacred Heart.

One last obstacle remained to be surmounted: Germaine was not yet 18, and so she would need the consent of her father. It seems that he who had formerly been so favorable to his daughter's wishes had changed his position—perhaps on account of his own plans concerning Germaine. He responded that he would have to see; he needed to consult Lucie and would act on her advice. Germaine experienced a moment of anguish: would she ever reach her goal?

Lucie hastened to write to her father, but he was going to be difficult. He demanded that Germaine first come to spend some time with him. She left for Bouchou, where she stayed a week. She slept on the floor on a blanket, for there was only one bed—and all day long she worked to persuade her father.

On the evening of her arrival they had stayed up visiting so late that midnight surprised them in the course of the conversation. Germaine, tired from her trip, wanted to go lie down. "My child," said Mr. Castang, "I never go to sleep without first having said my Rosary. This would be the first time I missed it since the death of your mother; would you like to say it with me?" They knelt down. "I remained there a long time," Germaine recounted, "for my dear Papa kept adding so many prayers to his Rosary that he never ended, and I fell asleep."

Germain Castang gave his daughter some lessons in devotion, and this one was particularly poignant. Despite his faults, he maintained a lively faith and a genuine piety.

At Nojals, Germaine once again visited her Uncle

Etienne, who, always so generous, agreed to pay her dowry for entrance to the monastery. Shortly afterward, having sent her rosary and First Communion medals to the Sisters of St. Joseph for Lucie, she said good-bye forever to the place of her childhood and, with an aching heart, left her father.

Mr. Castang, however, had not yet given his consent, and he now required that Germaine be photographed. We can certainly forgive him for this ingenious idea, since, thanks to him, we now possess the likeness of the holy young lady at that time. It is an interesting photograph which shows Germaine at the age of 18. She is wearing her boarding school uniform. (She took great care in her letters to point out that her Child of Mary ribbon, which looks white in the photo, is really blue.) Her countenance, plain and unshaken, with a somewhat childlike look, is nonetheless imprinted with a seriousness above her age. The attitude, the expression, the mouth firmly closed: all reveal a resolute and energetic character, but the energy is channeled, haloed by a strange serenity. Germaine's appearance is remarkably pure and pleasant, and her gaze, at once direct and distant, seems to be lost in contemplation while yet remaining attentive and ready for action. Martha and Mary in equal intensity united in one life: this is the perfect image of a soul who succeeded—at such a young age—in balancing the most difficult tension in the spiritual life: the harmonious joining of action and prayer without the loss of either. A touching detail: Germaine apparently neglected to arrange her hair before posing—typical of her who "never looked at herself."

Germaine speedily sent the photo to her father, begging him to hurry with his permission.

The precious letter finally arrived. Germaine was on her way! During the last weeks she spent at Nazareth she was radiant, smiling all the while as she worked. When she was asked the reason, she replied, "It seems to me that I am already in my little Poor Clare cell."

Once again the sweetness of this newfound joy would be tempered by painful affliction. During this time Germaine received a letter from Lucie which plunged her into a veritable anguish. We do not have this mysterious letter, and so we are left to conjecture about its contents.

What was happening? A variety of clues, including a later letter from Lucie and her subsequent life, allow us to reconstruct the facts fairly accurately. Lucie (Sr. Marie de St. Germain) was not happy at Aubenas. Teaching was beginning to weigh upon her, and she was becoming discouraged in the face of some problems that she was unable to overcome. She longed to leave the Congregation to enter a contemplative Order. In the end, this is exactly what she did; after having received a dispensation, she in turn went to knock on the doors of the Monastery of the Ave Maria, where she would end her days.

One last bitterness was dealt to Germaine on the eve of her departure. "All my dreams are being fulfilled," she would write on May 16: "a brother restored to my affection, and the religious life to which I aspired so ardently; my joy is complete." This brother was Guilbert, who had returned from Madagascar.

One day Guilbert's visit was announced to Germaine, and she ran to the parlor, eager to embrace him. She found the young soldier irritated and unhappy. He could not understand why she was leaving her family to go lock herself up in the cloister. To him this was unacceptable, and he begged her to renounce her plans. "My friend," responded Germaine, who in the face of this diatribe had found her own calm energy, "I did not prevent you from leaving for Madagascar, and you will not prevent me from going to the convent. You are free to follow the career you want, and I am free to follow my vocation."

This painful scene was the last contact Germaine had with her family, and it served to detach her from the world. On returning from the parlor she possessed her habitual pleasantness, as though her brother had simply embraced her.

∽ Chapter 3 ∾

Daughter of Saint Clare

At the Monastery

THE MONASTERY of the Ave Maria of Talence was brand new when Germaine entered. The Poor Clare Colettines from Grenoble had moved in during 1893, and the arrangement of the convent was still in process.

The monastery was modest and poor, as a convent should be. Nevertheless, the cloister arches, the red brick and whitewashed walls, the flowers and the clean newness of the building gave it a gay and pleasing appearance, conformable to the souls inhabiting it. The common rooms opened into the cloister: the chapter room, the refectory, the community room and the novitiate common room. On the upper floor, the doors of the identical cells lined the whole length of the corridor, and their small windows looked out over the courtyard. The monastery also had a garden which was cultivated by the Sisters.

Mother Claire-Isabelle, the Abbess, was sixty-eight years old, and this was not her first foundation. She was a superior of great wisdom, a big heart and very maternal goodness. At its beginning the new community numbered only six Sisters, but postulants were not long in coming.

On the afternoon of June 12, 1896, the Feast of the Sacred Heart, Germaine said her farewells at Nazareth and started off toward the place of her dreams. The little group that accompanied her included the Mother assistant, Sr. Noemi, the directress of the workroom, Claire, Joanès, and two other children. Germaine felt as though she had wings and forgot to limp.

They were welcomed with joy by their old friends, the extern Sisters. Then the group went to wait by the enclosure door. After an enormous key turned the lock, the Abbess embraced Germaine and presented her to the Mistress of Novices, Mother Seraphine, who in turn introduced her to the religious. Each one of the Sisters embraced her and said: "May God grant you peace and perseverance, dear Sister." After that, the doors closed once again, and the community, with the Cross leading them, processed through the cloister singing the Magnificat.

Germaine was led to the chapter room, where she was clothed in a black robe with a white gimp and a black veil with a white band, the dress of a postulant. Then it was on to the novitiate common room. There she was introduced to a diminutive nun with a pale but bright face illuminated by two large blue eyes, who was to be her "good angel" by helping to initiate her into the customs of the monastery. The Sister's name was Sr. Marie Pia. These two holy young souls were kindred spirits made for one another.

Germaine was shown to her cell—the happy little cell so long desired: only 3-1/2 x 2 meters, with four white walls, a hay mattress on a wooden board, a kneeler, a wooden cabinet, a basin and pitcher, a large crucifix and a holy water font. From her little window Germaine could see the cloister walk and the chapel bells. What peace!

Then she heard the bell ring for the first time, and Sr. Marie Pia conducted her to the choir. It was the hour of Vespers. After Vespers, the tabernacle doors were opened, and for an hour she was able to adore Jesus in the Blessed Sacrament exposed in the monstrance.

Germaine let herself be led from one place to another with the joyous indifference of one for whom everything is equally welcome, watching the succession of these exercises as so many parts in a beautiful symphony. At midnight, at the sound of the clapper, she arose for the office of Matins.

Already an entire day had flown by since Germaine had stepped over the threshold of the monastery door, and it had been nothing but a feast! But the religious life is a battle, as the little postulant was soon to learn.

The Battle Begins

Four days later, Germaine met a novice in the cloister and made a sign to her that she had something to say. "Listen," she said, "when I went to say good-bye to my father, people said 'Germaine is entering the convent. How pious she looks. . . . She's a little saint'— and here I find that I am already so full of faults!"

This was said with such a simplicity, candor and evident sincerity that the novice was deeply moved. What a transformation in just four days! With what generosity the young postulant must have corresponded with grace! From this day on, the novice had a deep respect for Germaine.

After three months, Germaine was astonishingly changed. She drew the admiration of all. Often there is a fiery fervor in postulants which superiors well know does not last. But here there was, without doubt, something that was solid and very serious.

Such precociousness in religious perfection is rare. But Germaine's whole life had been a preparation for this. She had entered the convent with a great and deep love already in her heart, as well as a strong habit of self-sacrifice. "I do not want to be a religious by halves," she had said before entering the convent. It seems that she kept her word with heroic courage.

The Taking of the Habit

Toward the end of October, 1896, the Mother Abbess gathered the community in chapter to vote on the admission of Germaine—"Sister Lucia"—to investiture.

The poor child was full of anguish. She was so convinced that she was worth nothing and that she "did everything wrong" that she seriously feared being sent away. While the Sisters were voting, she went to take refuge at the feet of the Blessed Virgin, and there begged her "good Mother" to have compassion on her.

It was in front of the statue of Our Lady that the Sisters found Germaine and announced to her the happy news of her reception. As they lead her to the chapter room, she was radiant and trembling with emotion. She thanked the Reverend Mother and the community with so much humility and gratitude that it brought tears to their eyes.

The clothing was set for November 21. Germaine made her preparation by a three-day retreat, of which her journal has been preserved.

Germaine did not sleep the night that preceded the "big day." She later remarked, "How long that night seemed!"

It is the custom of the Poor Clares for a postulant to assist at Mass dressed in secular garb with her family in the public chapel before the clothing. But because of her infirmity and in accord with her desire, Germaine remained within the enclosure. Besides, she had no family member present. Something that the Congregation did not know—apart from a few friends of the Monastery—was that the Sisters of Nazareth and the boarders of the orphanage had taken up a collection for candies, at great sacrifice, to offer to Lucia on the day of her investiture.

It was the Feast of the Presentation, and after the Mass, during which the boarders had sung one of Germaine's favorite hymns, she was led to the chapter room. There the Abbess cut her hair, took off her white dress and clothed her with the rough habit, cord, white veil and mantle of a Poor Clare novice.

Germaine then returned to the choir in her new livery and, amid her singing Sisters, knelt before the grille. The celebrant approached and said: "In the world you were called Mademoiselle Germaine Castang; in religion you will be called Sister Marie Celine of the Presentation."

It was with a radiant countenance that Sister Marie Celine went around to each Sister to receive the kiss of peace. Then she went to the parlor to greet her friends from Nazareth. She found real enjoyment amid her old friends, and she had some gracious little word for each of them. Just a little later, in the middle of recreation, while all were celebrating, she was suddenly struck by a strange sickness and had to leave the room. She felt faint, but merely said with a beautiful smile on her pale face, "Oh! It is nothing, just a bit of fatigue."

The victim had already been struck the fatal blow.

∽ Chapter 4 ∽

The Holocaust*

The Response to God

N O ONE had taken seriously this first symptom of the illness of Sr. Marie Celine. All believed, naturally, that it was due to the fatigue of the long ceremonies and the deep emotion of the day. She herself did not seem to see this illness for what it was, and her life continued as before, only with more fervor and a far greater attention to doing things well.

Had there been any suspicion of the seriousness of the illness which threatened Sr. Marie Celine, she would have been put into the infirmary immediately and ordered to take complete bed rest and extra nutrition. But the early symptoms of the disease are insidious and could pass for fatigue: a bit of cough; a slight fever which passes unnoticed. There follows the general decline of health and a depression which increases rapidly. It was in this state that Sr. Marie Celine con-

---

* In the Old Testament, a *holocaust* was an animal sacrifice that was completely consumed by fire. The word *holocaust* is also used to refer to the complete self-sacrifice to God that is made by a person who enters religious life, that is, a person who makes the vows of poverty, chastity and obedience.—*Publisher.*

tinued to follow the rigorous life of the Poor Clares, with the nocturnal hours, bare feet in the cold, abstinence and continual sacrifice which are required by the Holy Rule.

Sr. Marie Celine took no notice of her unusual fatigue, for this courageous young girl paid little attention to herself!

She was nominated surveillant of the novitiate. This duty, which would cost her so much and which seemed to her to be an "impossible task," she discharged wholeheartedly because it was the will of God. And she did it to perfection.

She who never looked around and had never wanted to concern herself with what others did, compelled herself to come out of the "enclosed garden" to watch everything, assess everything and correct her Sisters each time her duty called for it.

She had exercised this role already at Nazareth, and before that, with her little brothers and sisters. She was an expert at it and knew that sometimes severity was necessary. She surprised her companions with the categorical little tone she knew how to use when the occasion called for it, for they did not know it was in her.

She suffered especially from the lack of respect shown to superiors, for she herself felt for them such veneration, affection and a childlike confidence.

It would be altogether false to represent Sr. Marie Celine with a rigid and haughty air. She was gaity personified. Her heart had dilated in her beloved monastery. "Mother," she wrote, "at Nazareth they would never recognize me! I was so quiet and serious in comparison to what I am now! Here I have found what I was looking for . . . I am too happy!"

This cry of joy is quite moving, especially when one considers that a fatal disease had already taken hold of Sr. Marie Celine and, under subtle appearances, was progressing rapidly. It was winter, and she was quickly beginning to feel run-down.

One day the Mother Mistress, on entering Sr. Marie Celine's cell, found her alarmingly pale. "Mother, I cannot go on! I am suffering so much!" she exclaimed, as she threw herself into her Mistress's arms.

When the Mother Mistress heard of the symptoms afflicting Sr. Marie Celine, she had no doubt about the nature of the illness: it was consumption (tuberculosis) in its most brutal form.

The next day, the doctor was called. He declared: "She is lost. It's a matter of a few months. . . . She has had the illness in its germ for several years," he added.

In her overwhelming physical weakness, with her body tortured by pain, Sr. Marie Celine was suddenly drained of all energy; not even her mind served her any longer. Inert and without resistance, all she could do was suffer, crying like a baby in too much pain. In times when suffering passes beyond the limit of man's endurance, the soul, prostrate, seems to withdraw and leave free reign to nature. A wave of sadness descended upon the infirm little Sister, engulfing her without her being able to defend herself.

The Virtues of the Sick Novice

Sr. Marie Celine's first trial was having to renounce, for the most part, the conventual life to which she longed to be faithful. For the first few weeks she was still permitted to assist at some of the exercises; she followed the prayers of the Divine Office in choir, but without singing, and attended the conferences given by her Novice Mistress. Many things, however, were refused her, and she would be sent away to rest on her couch. How that cost her!

She humbly complained that she was kept from the work of a novice or the choir. "Dear Mother," she said one afternoon, "it seems to me that I am not so ill that I cannot rise at the sound of the bell in the morning. Couldn't I go to prayers?" One night, after Compline, a Sister found her in choir so worn out and in such great pain that she could barely hold herself up. She approached Sr. Celine, saying, "Our Mother must think you are lying down; will you go? You are very tired." "I have permission to stay just until eight," Sr. Celine responded sweetly, and she returned to her prayer. In seeing her pray, the other Sister was so vividly struck that she herself entered into fervent prayer.

At the beginning of her illness, Sr. Celine suffered from severe anguish fearing she would be sent home, for it is not customary to keep sick novices. One day a violent coughing fit made it necessary for her to leave the refectory. Mother Seraphine followed her out. The little one was crying; she asked, "What is the community supposed to do with a subject who is always ill?" The Mother Mistress, understanding her fear, responded, "You are afraid that we will not take care of you? But I assure you that you will stay here. Our good Mother Abbess does not want you to be cared for anywhere but here in the Monastery, and I shall be your nurse."

Sr. Celine had always found it so natural to be the servant of all, so it was a heavy trial for her to see herself surrounded by so much care and attention.

It is a remarkable fact that the Novice Mistress herself would consult Sr. Celine on difficult matters, without letting this be detected, finding in this young novice surprising insight and soundness of judgment.

In the Infirmary

Toward the end of 1896, Sr. Celine's conditioned worsened. On January 3, 1897, it was necessary for her to be moved from her cold, cramped cell, which was not airy enough, to the infirmary. She was settled in a room with two windows overlooking the garden and having its own fireplace.

This pleasant and bright room soon became for Sr. Celine an oratory and a sanctuary. Since it was Christmastime, a little crib was set up in her room. Mother Seraphine once surprised her as she was sitting on a little bench bouncing the figurine of the Infant Jesus on her knee, caressing Him, contemplating Him and speaking sweetly to Him.

Before and after Matins, someone would check on Sr. Marie Celine. One night, upon returning from choir, the Sister found her visibly shaken. "Would you remain with me for a half hour?" Sr. Celine asked. "I am afraid."

On the days she felt less fatigued she would still rise to attend Mass and receive Holy Communion. From there she would go to the novitiate common room for the morning spiritual exercises, which she would follow from her couch. But the days became more and more frequent when fatigue forced her to remain in the infirmary.

One day the Cardinal Archbishop of Bordeaux came to visit Sr. Celine. She received this visit with a grace and veneration that were charming. "Dear Mother," she said to her Novice Mistress, "it's incredible how distracted I was today. When I wanted to think of the Good God, I had so many distractions, I thought of the fire burning in the fireplace instead."

During his second visit, the Cardinal Archbishop announced his authorization for Sr. Celine to make her profession *in extremis,* when the superiors saw fit. Sr. Celine's white cheeks blushed with joy. "Oh, thank you, Your Eminence!" she exclaimed. She would die as a professed religious! She did nothing but prepare herself with a growing desire for this double event.

Anointing and Religious Profession

In the course of the month of March, the illness seemed to progress at an alarming pace.

On the night of the 20th, Sr. Celine was so gravely enfeebled that her death was thought to be imminent. The Sisters noticed that her feet were very swollen— a symptom which, according to the doctor, signified that the end was near.

At about one o'clock in the morning, the Novice Mistress told Sr. Celine that she was to be anointed and make her religious vows the following day. Her face lit up. Sr. Celine wanted this day to be a most beautiful holiday. The novices set to work, and at midday the infirmary was ravishingly beautiful. Garlands of white roses cascaded down the walls, forming a sort of canopy over the bed of Sr. Marie Celine, which was placed at the feet of the statue of the Immaculate Conception. On a white altar covered with flowers, the tabernacle of which held the Divine Host and was crowned with the statue of the Infant of Prague, were placed the black veil, the crucifix and the ring of profession.

At recreation time the religious came to pay her a visit, and some could not hold back their tears.

"Oh, my dear Sisters!" cried Sr. Celine. "Please do not cry, do not spoil my joy!"

Toward two o'clock in the afternoon, Sr. Celine saw Fr. Thaddée enter her room with the Blessed Sacrament, escorted by the community. After she had received Holy Viaticum, the novices sang, at her request, the hymn from the day of her First Holy Communion: "Behold the Lamb so sweet. . . ." Then she received the anointing with a happy smile.

The profession was made following a very simple rite. Fr. Thaddée preceded it by commenting on the verse in the Psalms: "Who will give me, O God, the wings of a dove, that I may fly away and be at rest?"

Sr. Marie Celine placed her folded hands into those of the Abbess and pronounced with a clear and calm voice her vows of obedience, poverty, chastity and enclosure. From the lips of the Superior fell these words: "And I, on the part of Almighty God, promise you everlasting life, if you observe these things." What a sweet promise for one at the close of her life, about to receive her recompense!

The ceremony ended, and the good Fr. Thaddée addressed to Sr. Marie Celine these words: "Now, my dear Sister, you must be resigned to the will of God; and if He wishes to heal you, you must want this also."

A Good Religious

Sr. Marie Celine seemed to have forgotten that she was ill, in her care to attend to the responsibilities of her profession. On the following day she asked to be kept informed of the novitiate conferences and the special announcements which are given daily to the junior professed Sisters.

The Reverend Mother and the Sisters were left to guess her needs and the cravings and repugnances of her poor stomach. They took pains in questioning her that they might learn of her discomforts and what could possibly be agreeable to her, but to whatever was offered her, she responded invariably with the same gracious "Thank you."

The invalid could hardly bear to take any food anymore, and the Sisters tried ingenious ways to discover her longings. "Is there anything you fancy?" asked Mother Seraphine one day. "Oh! One thing appeals to me," said Sr. Celine, "but it is useless to say, for at this moment you could not give them to me." "At least have the simplicity to tell me," said Mother Seraphine. Sr. Celine then admitted that for some time the only thing that she had desired to eat was a few strawberries.

The next day the good Mother Abbess had the extern Sisters search the city, and that evening the consumptive Sister was presented with five large, juicy strawberries. Sr. Celine was confounded.

"I'll be going to Purgatory for these strawberries," she said. "I cannot eat them with tranquility!"

"Be assured that you have performed an act of obedience in expressing to me your desire," said her Mother Mistress, "and you will do another in eating this fruit. The rest is our good Mother's business."

"Oh," added the Abbess, who was present, "to relieve a suffering Sister I would sell the sacred vessels without a scruple!"

Sr. Celine, with peace restored, ate the strawberries but begged her superiors not to repeat such "follies," as it tried her love of holy poverty.

The Mother Abbess, who was almost seventy and afflicted with severe rheumatism, could no longer bend down, but she often knelt near the sickbed to care for Sr. Marie Celine. It was moving to see the venerable Superior kneeling before the little infirm Sister, forgetting her own pains to bring some relief by her maternal love.

A few days later, Sr. Celine sent to Sr. Marie de St. Germain one last note in poor, trembling penmanship:

> "My dear little sister, I am so happy. If soon you hear the news of my death, be at peace, I am dying happy. The day of my death will be the most beautiful for me.
>
> > Your little sister,
> > Celine"

For her father, she dictated a longer letter:

> ". . . I am going to leave this earth to go to Heaven. Think how up there I will not forget you, so that this news does not sadden you too much! Dear Papa, I am going happily, surrounded by a million attentions from our Reverend Mothers."

She went on to tell him about the strawberries, which had been brought to her at the cost of 35 cents each.

> "As I no longer had the strength to raise my hand to my mouth, my two Mothers fed me themselves like their little baby. Unite yourself with me to thank the Good God for having given me such good Mothers.

"Farewell, dear Papa. I embrace you with all my heart and ask that you not be disturbed on my account. Your little daughter who loves you and who is leaving the world without regret, having sacrificed to God all that she held dearest on earth.

"We will meet again in Heaven! Farewell.

Sr. Celine"

The Smile amid Tears

Sr. Celine's poor body was devoured by fever, her lungs were lacerated by constant coughing, her throat was on fire, her stomach had shut down and she could no longer either eat or sleep. Her feet were swollen and the wound in her leg reopened. Day and night she was tormented without a moment's respite. A new wave of heaviness descended upon her soul in its disarray. "Oh, Mother," she cried out one evening, "what sadness to think I will soon leave my Mother and Sisters! The pain is too great to bear; I want to cry, but I can't. I have never known happiness here on earth except since my entrance here, and how short have I been able to rejoice! Oh, Mother, do you think that I have no sorrow in my heart at leaving all of you?" And in her voice there was a veritable distress.

Holy Week was terrible. Jesus generously allowed Sr. Celine to share in His Passion. Her illness suddenly took a turn for the worse, and at that point they were persuaded that she would not last till Easter. Nevertheless, she did hear the Easter bells pealing.

Beginning on May 3, the Feast of the Finding of the True Cross, her condition worsened, her sufferings became intolerable, and from one moment to the next they expected to see her expire.

One day she suffered on account of the nurse's over-sight—it is known how painful these negligences are to a sick person—but Sr. Marie Celine said nothing. "Why did you not say something?" asked Mother Seraphine. "I am a Poor Clare and ought to mortify myself. A religious should never protest." Never did she request any care or relief. Her daily nourishment was half of an apricot and two or three strawberries.

The Final Combats

There have been testimonies that the Monastery of the Ave Maria had filled with mysterious perfumes. Whatever the case, these heavenly graces, which sweet-ened the last days of the little dying Sister, were like the Angel of Gethsemane: nothing but a tonic to sus-tain her in her last combats.

Fr. Thaddée had told her one day that he would come on the morrow to hear her Confession. "What should I tell him?" she asked her Novice Mistress; "I have nothing to say." Shortly after, she added: "Alas! The just sin seven times a day; and I? I am so blind that I do not see my sins!"

She had always been very candid with her spiritual director and brief in her Confessions. She was a per-son who never complicated matters, and she was too little interested to speak very long of herself.

On May 29, toward nine o'clock in the evening, alarming symptoms appeared. Without the possibility of doubt, this was the end. The prayers for the dying were begun. Then Sr. Celine begged pardon of her Sis-ters for all the pains she had caused them . . . but in reality, the first pain she would cause them would also be the last: that of dying. At ten o'clock, she looked at her two Mothers with an inexpressible tenderness. "I cannot cry," she said to them, "but it truly is hard to leave you." Then she closed her eyes, kissed her crucifix in a gesture of love and entered into a great silence. A few hours later she expired.

It was Sunday, May 30, 1897 at three o'clock in the morning.

"I Will Forget No One"

In the morning, the nuns were awakened to the sound of the *De Profundis* (*Psalm* 129 [130]), which announced the passing of their little Sister. They all quickly gathered around the bed on which she reposed.

They could not stop contemplating the dear remains which the soul had left so beautiful and eloquent, haloed in her aura.

In the afternoon the body was prepared for viewing. Sr. Celine's head lay on a bundle of vine branches, according to the Poor Clare custom, and she was taken to the choir.

The coffin was left open, and the friends of Sr. Marie Celine and of the monastery were able to see her through the grille. All received the same impression: a reflection of heavenly glory seemed to emanate from her serene countenance.

The next day, a small funeral procession formed: the extern Sisters, a few friars, representatives from the Refuge of Nazareth, and a small group of the faithful. The mortal remains of the little Sr. Marie Celine were brought to the cemetery of Talence. The grain of wheat must fall to the earth and die in order to produce much fruit.

Those who knew the "little saint" did not delay in invoking her, for they felt more drawn to pray *to* her than *for* her. It was beginning to be discovered that Sr. Marie Celine was keeping her promise: "I will forget no one," and that her merits were great before God.

The grave of Sr. Marie Celine soon became a place of pilgrimage. On some days it would even disappear beneath the flowers which were laid upon it. Accounts of favors received began pouring in by the hundreds. An informative process was opened, and in 1930, the Cause of Beatification was officially introduced to the court in Rome.

In 1927, Sister Celine's body had been exhumed and transferred to a vault. Later, her remains were restored to the Monastery of the Ave Maria.

On June 25, 1980, the body of Sr. Marie Celine was moved to the new Monastery of the Poor Clares in Fontaudin-Pessac.

In 2006, affected by the lack of new vocations, the Poor Clares left Pessac and were welcomed by their Sisters in Nieul sur Mer, France. At this time it was decided that the remains of Sister Marie Celine should be moved to her native village of Nojals. Thus on June 26, 2006, early in the morning, in the presence of her Poor Clare Sisters, some priest friends of the monastery, the Sisters of St. Joseph and a few close friends, the remains of Sister Marie Celine were exhumed and placed in a pure white coffin. Her body was buried in the church of Nojals, at the foot of the altar, facing the Blessed Sacrament. There visitors may come and confide to her their special intentions.

On January 22, 1957, after a long process of detailed inquiries, the Holy Father Pope Pius XII had solemnly declared the heroicity of the virtues of this Servant of God in these words:

> "It is evident that Marie Celine of the Presentation practiced to a heroic degree the theological virtues of faith, hope, and charity, both with regard to God and toward her neighbor, as well as the cardinal virtues of prudence, justice, temperance and fortitude, with the other contingent virtues."

With that declaration the Servant of God became known as "Venerable." For over 50 years the saintly Poor Clare was called "Venerable Marie of the Presentation."

Then on September 16 of 2007, to the great joy of Poor Clares everywhere, Sister Marie Celine was beatified by Pope Benedict XVI, thus being accorded the title of "Blessed."

PART TWO

"A Lily of the Cloister"

A Lily of the Cloister

The following material regarding Sr. Celine's life as a Poor Clare was adapted from a booklet by Rev. J. A. Shields, B.D., L.C.L. (Maynooth), which in turn drew from biographical material composed by Sr. Marie Celine's Novice Mistress.

The Better Part

IT MIGHT be well to say a few words here on the privileged life of the Poor Clare. Within the enclosure she is vowed to perpetual prayer and fasting and every kind of penance. She sings the Divine Office and watches through the night hours: praying for those who sleep, for those who suffer and for poor sinners, praying for the world's sanctification and for an increased love for her Divine Spouse. The scanty rest she takes is on a hard bed of straw. Her feet are bare. No ordinary vocation has led her to the cloister. She is vowed to an existence the hidden mystery of which will only be known beyond the grave.

Here on earth it all seems so strange and incomprehensible. If we could but imagine the wonderful results of her prayers—those prayers mingled as they are with blood and tears. Could we but finger the links of the mysterious chain which, in the cloister, binds together things spiritual and material and experience the revelations, the visions and the sweet perfumes. But the Poor Clares resemble other holy Orders in that

75

they do not whisper to the world at large of the joys which, even here below, God has been pleased to bestow on them. We must not try to penetrate into their seraphic secrets.

As for Jeanne-Germaine, her own purpose was: "I shall succeed, God willing. As we are going to God, it is better to give ourselves entirely to Him." And now we enter on a new phase of her life.

Love and Sacrifice

Within the cloister Germaine immediately set to work to become a true religious. To the Novice Mistress she offered herself very generously to be corrected of all her imperfections and to be taught how to become a saint. She admitted that she did not like humiliations, but she was anxious to learn to love them, and her indomitable will conquered all and gained her even this. From then on her humility was admirable; she judged herself unworthy to live with her companions who were so pious and so good. Her greatest pleasure was to be ignored; mortification and renunciation spoke lovingly to her heart, and both she sought and cherished. In like manner did she feel toward holy poverty.

On one occasion, Germaine obediently left her cell untidy in order to hurry off punctually to the chapel for the scheduled visit to the Blessed Sacrament. Upon her return, the cell was in perfect order, yet no human hand had touched it. The Reverend Mother concluded that Germaine's Guardian Angel was responsible.

After Germaine's death the novices were told how God had thus mysteriously rewarded her exact obedience, and the cell that had once been hers was named by her Sisters, *"The cell set in order by the Angels."*

The Novice Mistress recounted, "And all the time Germaine was never content to offer less than full measure to Our Lord. In a few months she had grasped the vital law of the *Agere Contra* ["To act against" one's inclinations]. What she was forbidden to do in external penances on account of her tender age and delicate health she more than made up for by interior self-immolation. And so she proceeded on the way of perfection, gathering strength and beauty as she went along."

Sister Marie Celine, Novice

Germaine's Clothing on November 21 was preceded by a three-day retreat. Witness her resolutions: "Interior silence—shunning all useless thoughts. Obedience—prompt, blind. Humility—profound.

"When I quit my worldly garb I will pray that all vain thoughts may vanish from my heart and that I may become truly religious. When I don the garb of a Poor Clare I will beg Jesus to loose me from the chains of earth and bind me to Himself with the chains of Divine Love. As I put on the veil I will beg Him to hide me from the world—I will live a hidden life in God."

Germaine further resolved to pray frequently to St. Aloysius Gonzaga and to spend a few minutes each day in meditating on Hell; finally, with praiseworthy exactitude, she closed her retreat with a list of the faults committed by her as a postulant, and she also counted up all her acts of self-sacrifice. But Germaine's faults were, in reality, the merest imperfections. The community, from the Very Reverend Mother Abbess down to the youngest postulant, declared that not only was the dear child never seen to commit a venial sin, but there was never in her any manifestation of voluntary imperfection.

On November 21, the Feast of the Presentation, Germaine became a novice. She seemed so joyous on that happy day. Germaine's little friends chanted their sweetest songs, and the holy community, intoning the Psalm, *Quam dilecta tabernacula tua, Domine*—"How lovely are Thy tabernacles, O Lord"—led their darling child to the chapter room, there to receive in solemn function the habit of their holy Order. Germaine did not tremble when her beautiful hair was cut off; and when the coarse serge habit of the Order was laid on her shoulders, she smiled and whispered to the Divine Bridegroom her touching little prayer that mortification and penance might clothe her within as the religious habit clothed her outwardly. She received the long white veil which was henceforth to hide her from the world; she tied around her waist the Franciscan cord; finally, upon her humble brow was placed the crown of thorns. At the conclusion of the ceremony Germaine, bearing a large crucifix, was conducted in procession back to the choir, led by the Very Reverend Mother Abbess and the Novice Mistress. She came to the grille and was thus addressed:

"In the world your name was Jeanne-Germaine Castang; your name in religion is Marie Celine of the Presentation." The new novice chanted in reply: *"Gaudens, gaudebo in Domino, quia induit me vestimentis salutis, sicut Sponsam ornatem monilibus suis"*—"With joy I rejoice in the Lord because He has clothed me in the garments of salvation, as a bride adorned with her jewels." The deed was done. There was now no Germaine, but Sister Marie Celine taking her place among the novices of St. Clare.

Full and sweet came her Sisters' reply: *"Ecce quam bonum et quam jucundum habitare fratres in unum"*— "Oh how good and joyful it is when brothers dwell together as one." Community life is, in very truth, sweet and joyful. Before quitting the choir the new novice signed the deed of her clothing. She had already renounced herself completely, and her oblation was soon to be accepted. Happy are those who know how to storm the fortress of Divine Love and to offer themselves absolutely and forever.

The Harvest

Sr. Marie Celine's was an ideal example. The private diaries of all the novices strike the same note of admiration for their perfect little Sister. She was indeed a model of charity, humility, unselfishness and external observance. But it must not be imagined that she was morbid or gloomy. In point of fact she became, as time went on, much more cheerful than she had been when she first entered the cloister. Love, joy and peace frequently go together, and Sr. Marie Celine in her pure, innocent happiness was the life and soul of the hours of recreation. She was absolutely at home and at peace with the whole community. "Dear Mother," she said one day to the Novice Mistress, "they would not know me now at Nazareth" (where she had stayed with the Sisters of the Presentation). "I used to be so silent and quiet there. Now I am my real self and in my right place. I have found all that I wanted: I am too, too happy." She was ever most touching grateful and sweetly affectionate. She often used to say: "Our dear Reverend Mother Abbess had the great charity to receive me. How grateful I must be to her for so much kindness toward me! How I love her! How much I should like to show my gratitude in every way."

But again, she was anything but feeble or weak, and could on occasion be quite severe. One day a postulant asked her an unnecessary question during the hours of silence. "I must not speak now," she answered, "and besides, I am not going to discuss my personal affairs at any time." And away she went, leaving her questioner quite dumbfounded. Sometimes, indeed, her strict silence was almost too much for new postulants. However, they were very careful not to break the Rule in her presence—they knew well that the slightest breach of any observance of it caused real pain to her sensitive soul. She could not understand how anyone could think of trying to evade authority, or be in any way deceitful or shuffling. Loving and charitable though she was, she showed pleasure when once the Novice Mistress dismissed a postulant of whom she could not feel exactly sure.

And this is her picture as a novice: humbly convinced of her own nothingness, affectionate to her Sisters, loving respectful and grateful to her Reverend Mothers and an obedient child to them; firm as a rock to any postulant who tried to evade the rules, mortified, punctual, simple, sincere, always forgetful of self and esteeming herself the very least of all.

The Trial

Sr. Marie Celine was advancing rapidly in the mysterious ways of holiness, but her frail body, alas, was visibly declining. Her Novice Mistress, noticing her extreme pallor, counselled with the Reverend Mother Abbess, and the doctor was sent for. He examined Sr.

Marie Celine and said at once: "No hope whatever, she will only last a few months or so." It was consumption, and there is no doubt that the disease had been latent for long, though hitherto she had seemed so well and so free from pain. And all the time the dear child had bravely struggled on. Her patience was to be brought to the highest pitch in her *fiat* ("Let it be done") for physical pain. Neither suffering nor death frightened her, but as she was to have her own Gethsemane, hours of bitter agony awaited her.

At first the care taken of the dear little invalid wounded her great humility. "I ought to serve others instead of being the object of everyone's care and attention," she used to say; and when she feared to be too spoiled, she was advised to accept in a spirit of humility all that was done for her. Sr. Celine promised that she would, but it is easy to understand that she would have preferred a good humiliation to all the attentions that were given her.

For a few weeks she continued to say prayers with the community. She was there for Divine Office, and although she could no longer sing, she followed the exercises of the novitiate and eagerly hoped to glean humiliation there. But with what could the angelic child be reproached? This world was not pure enough for her pure soul. Ill and feeble though she was, she always wanted to be occupied and would beg to be allowed to take her part in the work allotted to the novices. She disliked being made an exception, though she always smilingly and gracefully obeyed when told to cease any fatiguing employment.

Toward the end of January of this year (1897) she became much weaker, and a new vista of holiness opened up before her. Hitherto she had bravely met illness, misfortune, loss of loved ones, loneliness, penances and the thought of approaching death. Now she was to struggle against the powers of darkness and in humble imitation of her Divine Master she was to break the heavy yoke of the demon and overthrow his cruel scepter.

Struggle and Triumph

On the Feast of the Epiphany the invalid was moved from her little cell—the cell set in order by the Angels— into a large, airy room, specially prepared and arranged to appease her longings for solitude and prayer. And now she soon reached a stage when she thought of nothing but of Him who was the Lord of her soul. Any distraction was not merely a subject of reproach but of astonishment to her. To her Novice Mistress she said one night: "Mother, it is extraordinary that I should have been so distracted all day today. I was quite unable to think of God when I wished to do so!" And what were these distractions? When queried she replied: "I kept on thinking of the fire as it crackled in the fireplace." Such were the distractions with which she reproached herself.

And now the arch-enemy of souls, aroused by her innocent perfection, soon began to try his strength against her. One night while the Community was in the chapel praying *Matins,* Sr. Celine was alone in her room. When, after choir, one of the lay Sisters went to see if she wanted anything, she said: "Stay here, stay half an hour at least, I am frightened." The Sister stayed, of course, and little by little Sr. Celine became quite calm and dismissed her cheerfully. The next day she told the Novice Mistress of all the terrors she had endured. The devil had assailed her. However, a few nights later, the disturbance occurred once more. She heard such terrible sounds that she almost fainted from fright, and next morning she literally wept with terror when she told her dear Novice Mistress what had happened. Henceforth it was decided that someone should stay with her. And soon, the Sister appointed to watch by Sr. Celine was a witness to the manifestations that occurred. If indeed it was the devil, his assaults against this faithful little friend of the Most High were all in vain. Sr. Marie Celine threw herself with absolute confidence into the extended arms of the Crucified, and was very courageous throughout all these severe trials.

Danger of death, however, did not as yet appear to be imminent, and Sr. Celine pursued the even tenor of her simple life as heretofore, rising for Holy Mass and assisting at the usual morning exercises of the novitiate, resting the while in her invalid chair. Her patience was most edifying. Never did she neglect the least requirement of the Rule unless prevented by her health. None who saw her, her hands clasped in prayer, will ever forget the perfect example she set by her fervor and her modesty. Every obeisance or act of reverence which the Rule prescribes was punctually made by her. Her attention never flagged at the spiritual readings and conferences. She truly hungered for all these things, and even after she had received the last rites, she begged that she might still be carried into the midst of the novices to enjoy her share of what she called "the banquet of their practices," and feast with them on the bread of humility and the fruit of obedience. With her poor little thread of a voice she still managed to humiliate herself vigorously. "I am quite without virtue," she said sometimes. "Oh, how it grieves me when others seem to think me good."

When all work was forbidden her, she lay motionless in her invalid chair, the crucifix in her clasped hands, her eyes closed, a smile always playing about her lips. She was now never left alone. She spoke but rarely, except to the Very Reverend Mother Abbess or the Mother Mistress. To them she opened her heart, speaking of Heaven, of the joys of Divine Love, of the infinite kindness of the Sacred Heart. The last entry in Sr. Celine's diary gives a glimpse into her heart: "My pen shakes as I write, my Jesus tries me by suffering. I have resolved that I will be a humble violet, a rose of love, a lily of purity—all for Jesus."

The Holy Vows

Sr. Celine longed to make her vows and then to be at rest forever in Heaven. Suffering here below was to her a sure guarantee of future joy above. By way of preparation for her vows she made a short retreat, during which she was very peaceful and very happy. And when the Novice Mistress announced to her that on the morrow her profession *in extremis* would take place and that she would also receive the Last Sacraments, her joy was touching to behold. "Oh, Mother," she whispered, "what glorious news. Tomorrow the Last Sacraments! My holy vows! Then to die! Oh, rapture, Heaven at last!" She tried to raise her feeble arms, she was so radiant with joy. And so she passed that night in prayer and in silent communing with the eternal Bridegroom who was to accept her espousals in the morning.

The next day the good Sisters prepared for the ceremony. It was like a Corpus Christi procession—unforgettably beautiful. The Gothic arches of the cloister were flooded with the sunshine and sweet scents of early spring. Jasmine, clematis, roses and honeysuckle seemed to be putting forth their fresh green buds in honor of the Blessed Sacrament, borne in procession. The veiled virgins, preceded by the great cross of wood, reciting the *Miserere;* the sons of St. Francis answering the Psalm; Our Lord Himself borne through the sunny cloister; the great statues of the Saints, mute witnesses of the procession; and high in the tower above, the birds warbling sweetly—it was indeed a touching, loving spectacle, and all hearts were filled with love and eyes with tears as they looked on.

Sr. Marie Celine herself looked like the marble recumbent effigy of a saint. Robed in her conventual garb, draped in the white veil so soon to be exchanged for the black one, she reclined peacefully smiling upon her white couch and clasped to her heart a great garlanded crucifix, to which had been affixed the formula of her holy vows—the contract of the mystical betrothal. She was confessed, communicated and anointed, and the ceremony of her profession began.

She looked entranced at the blessing of the crucifix, veil and ring. Calmly and distinctly she repeated the four great vows—poverty, chastity, obedience and enclosure—by which she became a professed nun of the Seraphic Order.* When she had finished, the Very Reverend Mother Abbess said: "I, in the name of God and according to His Holy Will, promise that if you

---

* "The Seraphic Order" is the Franciscan Order, the Order founded by St. Francis of Assisi, who was like a seraph—an angel of the highest choir—in his love for God. The Poor Clares are a branch of the Franciscan Order.—*Publisher*.

faithfully observe these vows, you will receive life eternal." And all the nuns answered: "Amen."

The ceremony continued. The holy Rule was handed over, the crucifix of profession presented, the ring of faith placed upon the right hand, and finally the white veil removed and replaced by the black. The choir then intoned the triumphant anthem of St. Agnes: *"Posuit signum in faciem meam ut nullam praeter eam amatorem admittam"*—"He hath set a seal upon my face that I should admit no other lover but Him." And in the evening followed the further touching ceremony of the consecration of the newly professed to the Blessed Virgin. Thus ended in all joy, peace and happiness an unforgettable day for Sr. Marie Celine of the Presentation and for the privileged community of the Ave Maria.*

Waiting for Heaven

Heaven was not, however, forthwith to open its everlasting gates to this dear soul. Some two months of suffering yet lay before her, and these last days were among the most touching and beautiful of her life. Her thoughts throughout were ever fixed on Heaven, and she tried to sanctify each moment of the days yet remaining to her.

She was determined to possess nothing at her death.

---

* In her diary on the same day she wrote: "I am so happy that I cannot tell of my good fortune . . . I am speechless before Your tabernacle, O my Divine Jesus, and in this powerlessness I say to You: 'Here I am, deprived of expressing all sentiments . . . I feel my great happiness and I cannot tell You of it—may my silence speak for me . . . or better, keep me in Your presence, like a little artificial flower, and I will be the ornament on Your altar.'"
—Quoted by Jeanne Briand in article "Along Unbeaten Paths to the Encounter with Sr. Celine," from the booklet *Marie Celine of Nojals at Pessac, 1878-1897*, Poor Clares of Fontaudin-Pessac.

One day she had the little box which contained all her letters, little pictures, etc., brought to her bedside. She then gave it, just as it was, to the Very Reverend Mother Abbess, saying: "Take it all, dear Mother, all of it." Her little intimate treasures all given away, she clasped her hands and looked upwards with the most angelic smile. She seemed to be saying: "I have nothing more on earth; I await eternal life."

Yes, she was indeed waiting and watching. The last days of struggle before the final victory were approaching. Suffering and feeble but strong in faith, hope and love, she was to be called upon to battle against temptations—against the old enemy himself. The old serpent had not yet surrendered. He was there near our dear little maiden, he snarled at her like a dog on a chain. But as St. Augustine says, he can bite only those who venture too near. He was able only to alarm Sr. Marie Celine—he never overcame her in the slightest degree. Our Lord was ever near her, saying: "Courage. I have overcome the world." Sometimes the dear child was much cast down, but the thought of Our Blessed Lady, Help of Christians, restored her on these occasions to her habitual calm and helped her surely to triumph over the powers of darkness.

But though our Sr. Marie Celine had her hours of sorrow and of mortal combat with these powers of darkness, she had also the most wonderful consolations. Just an instance: one day she felt a little stronger and had asked to be carried to the Community Room for the spiritual reading. Here she was almost overpowered with the most delicious heavenly perfumes. She could not imagine from whence the scent was coming, and thought that one of the nuns had some violets somewhere. There were, however, none to be seen. And the mystery remained unexplained. So between trials and consolations she passed her final period of waiting, and soon was to prepare to enter in radiance the abode of eternal glory.

Last Sufferings and Blissful Death

During the sunny, flowery month of May, Sr. Marie Celine was to drink the cup of suffering* to the very dregs. But she never murmured. Her one regret was

---

* We insert here some details set forth by a medical doctor who studied Sister Celine's life in the 1990's.—*Publisher.*

"On January 3, 1897, the illness became serious, and Sr. Celine was moved to the infirmary, to a larger and more airy room than her cell.

"During the night of March 20, 1897, it was believed she was on the point of death. It was noted that her feet were considerably swollen. It is possible that these edemas were due to an acute anemia.

"'Her poor body was nothing but suffering. Devoured by high fever, her lungs lacerated by her cough, her throat on fire, her stomach completely disordered, she could no longer neither eat nor sleep.'

"From May 3, the symptoms worsened further, 'her cough was continual, the fever devoured her, and acute chest pains tortured her, and she was suffocating.'

"On Monday, May 17, around 4 a.m., death was thought to have arrived. Both the confessor and the doctor were sent for, who could only confirm the immanence of death and withdraw, leaving her unconscious.

"On Wednesday, May 26, she suffered so intensely of fever and the sensation that her whole body was on fire that she asked: 'Mother, are morphine treatments costly?'

"On Sunday, May 30, 1897, at 3 a.m., she gave up her soul. Her human destiny, consumed by tuberculosis, was achieved."

> —From article "Marie Celine of the Presentation and the Doctor: A Century after Her Death," by Doctor Philippe Gosse-Gardet, from the booklet *Marie Celine of Nojals at Pessac, 1878-1897,* compiled by the Poor Clares of the Monastery of Fontaudin-Pessac.

that she was the cause of so much trouble and annoyance to others. And thus, hovering between life and death, she passed the days in prayer and silence, perfecting herself for the meeting with her Divine Spouse. Day by day she wondered when it was to be. Novenas had been made for her recovery, but that was not to come. On May 30 she entered on her agony and passed away in peace and joy to her Eternal Father. Let us describe the last moments of this blissful passing.

She had asked forgiveness for any trouble she had given, and then kissed her crucifix with supreme resignation. But then she suddenly became convulsed. With terror visible in her countenance, she cried: "I see the devil coming toward me!" The good Sisters tried to soothe her and comfort her, but Satan persisted in his attempts. However, kissing the crucifix again her radiant peace returned. And then came her reward. For shortly before her death, looking to her right she exclaimed: "Look at that Lady. Oh, isn't she lovely!" Three times she murmured ecstatically the same words, her eyes remaining fixed upon this celestial vision. "Don't you see that Lady over there? She is so lovely." Then she added suddenly: "Listen, there are bells ringing!" . . . and then, "So many little girls all in white." No doubt she beheld the procession of those who follow the Lamb. They were waiting there with Our Lady to receive the pure soul of the Bride of Christ.

Sr. Marie Celine raised herself on her pillow and from her heart arose the sweet murmuring of a prayer like the soft cooing of a dove; then, bowing her head on the right, she expired, clasped in the arms of her Very Reverend Mother Abbess and Mother Mistress.

She was just nineteen years and six days old. It was on Sunday at three o'clock in the morning. In the garden under the windows of her cell was a bed of budding lilies. One lovely bloom expanded just as Sr. Marie Celine passed from this earth. On the far horizon streaks of gold and purple heralded the dawn and looked like a glorious pathway leading from this vale of tears to the golden heights of Heaven. Facing the dawn, Sr. Marie Celine lay motionless. Jesus, the "Sun" of Glory, had arisen before her in divine Majesty. She had found her Beloved, she was safe with her Saviour and her Judge. She was radiant as a star. *"Fulgebunt justi et tanquam scintillae in arundineto discurrent"*—"The just shall shine, and shall run to and fro like sparks among the reeds." (*Wis.* 3:7).

God is admirable in His Saints.

* * * * *

Sr. Marie Celine's sanctity consisted not so much in any extraordinary works of exterior piety as in a quiet interior harmony with God's benign will. Her life has been written by her Novice Mistress, who had access to many intimate details otherwise unknown. This life, then, must remain for all time the standard record of her deeds. The present article has been compiled largely with its help and solely with a view to bringing before willing souls the light of a shining example and the incentive of a loving creed. It may help to make this little Sister better known and better loved, and so attain to God's glory in the interest of her cause. Meanwhile, in Holy Mother Church's keeping we leave her sacred memory.

PART THREE

Letters

Letters

"Unpublished" Letters of Sister Marie Celine from the Poor Clare Monastery of Pessac

Letter 1

(Note: This first letter cannot be from the pen of Germaine, for one cannot find the characteristic traits of her writing; besides, the edifying style is not that of the young girl, and the French spelling errors which are particular to her are missing.)

Bordeaux, January, 1893

Dear Papa,

In my thoughts I journey to the middle of the little cottage where I have left all that I loved. Yes, I seem to see you all alone, abandoned in this little cottage, sad and afflicted for having seen yourself once surrounded by so numerous a family and now alone, all alone in your poor little dwelling.

But dear Papa, we have a great hope in thinking that God in highest Heaven is watching over us. He has sent you some great trials; still, it is for us a proof of His love, to show us how much He loves us; and, dearest Papa, let us resign ourselves to His holy Will. He will not abandon us but will take us under His protection; He will follow each of our steps and preserve us, like the Angel preserved Tobias. Do not allow yourself to be forlorn; on the contrary, every morning arise stronger and more resigned, knowing that you are under the watchful care of God, who cannot abandon you. For all Christians must hope, so show yourself a valiant Christian and that you know how to fight with energy.

I am sure that God sees the great efforts you make, and He will repay you sooner or later, for God always rewards those who trust in Him.

Trust in God, dear Papa; have no hope but in Him alone, and count not on creatures, for tomorrow they change, but God is a faithful friend and happily He does not betray us.

You've known my desire for a long time, how I lean toward Jesus and how I languish in not being able to become His spouse. Well, dear Papa, I know you have consented long ago to this plan, but the Will of God comes before all else, and the rest follows. Guilbert wrote to me recently, he is doing very well. Our good Mother is always for us an Angel of little attentions, as are the Mistresses who care for the two little ones, making them a thousand times happy. I end my letter, dear Papa, with a heart full of hope.

Your child who loves you and always will,

Germaine Castang

Letter 2

(Note: Sometimes Germaine signs her letters "Lucia" instead of "Germaine." The reason for this is that upon her arrival at the Refuge of Nazareth she was given the name "Lucia" because there was already a little girl there named "Germaine.")

[1893?]

Dearly beloved Papa,

Do not ever be anxious, for you must know that we are here in safety of body and soul. Our good Mother is too attached to our family to allow us to suffer; we must pray Our Lord to preserve her a long time, as well as our good Mistress.

My little sisters are doing well, just I am a little fatigued. Good Sr. Noemi made me lie down on account of the wound on my leg. I cannot write more to you today, but I will write a longer letter later, for now I am in bed. I am happy to receive news of you. Let me hear from you as soon as you can.

The little ones embrace you with all their hearts, as do I, who pray to God for you.

Lucie, Lucia and Clothilde

Letter 3

Bordeaux, June 11, 1893

Dearly beloved Father,

I imagine my letter will find you greatly concerned over us, so I hasten to write to assure you that all three of us are in good health, only my leg is not yet healed.

I am not suffering, it is just annoying to always have this wound; but it is the Good God who wants His most holy Will to be done. I went to Lourdes with a heart overflowing with joy. I had hoped to be healed, but the Holy Virgin did not wish to obtain a miracle for me, doubtless because I was not indifferent enough. Oh, dear Papa, I cannot tell you how my heart swelled approaching the blessed grotto! I could not stop crying, and I knelt before the image which spread out before my eyes. Oh, I cannot describe that which passed within my soul when I saw all those crutches, when I saw the piety with which everyone was animated, when I saw the basilica where this tender Mother is venerated!

I did not know what to say before all the ex-voto ornaments with which the churches are decorated; they are but words of gratitude which one sees everywhere. Oh, how happy I would have been to be healed; I too would have said Thank You! But it was not so. I had had high expectations during the whole trip, and especially at the moment I immersed my leg into the pool, but evening came and I returned to Bordeaux as I had come. As for me, dear Papa, I think it is because of you that I was not healed, for finally I prayed, as best I could, and I told my Mother: "I love your divine Son Jesus, but I'd love Him even more if He healed me." I also said to my Mother: "Do not be insensitive to the prayers which I address to you; it is not only I who pray to you, but also all my Mistresses and all my companions. Ah no, my Mother, you cannot remain unmoved by all our supplications!" In spite of our prayers, the Mother of God did not bend. It seems like the hand of God weighs heavily upon me.

I'm going to write to Lucie today.

Guilbert wrote to me. He is in Oleron. He is bored but hopes to leave soon.

Our dear Mother is always good to us. I think she

will be very saddened when my little sisters leave.

Good Sr. Noemi is always for us the replacement of what we have lost, as are all of our Mistresses.

Clothilde and Lucie speak to me often of you and tell me you never come to see them. If you could come, I would be very happy too, and I would give you the rosary which I brought back from Lourdes and which I touched to the grotto.

Dear Papa, it remains only for me to tell you that we had the procession of the Blessed Sacrament last Sunday. Clothilde and Lucia were the two little flower girls, and I wished you had been there to see them. They were all curly like two little poodles.

No more to tell you for the moment, dear Papa.

Please give Levy a big hug for us.

> Your children who love you tenderly,
>
> Lucia Castang

Letter 4

(Note: This letter of Germaine was found on the road in Nojals by Madame Veuve Lagreze; she kept it until February 9, 1933.)

September 29, 1893

Dearly beloved Papa,

What a great joy I felt in receiving a letter from you, but also what grief of heart in realizing the few lines your hand wished to pen!

You tell me you are sick. I wondered if you had something when I didn't receive any news of you. At last, we must accept all from the divine Master!

You seemed surprised to hear of all that has happened to Lubine and Lucie.

My good Mistresses of Nojals wrote to me twice: the first time to announce that the Pastor was coming to Bordeaux and that on that same occasion they would bring our dear little angels.

The second time, they told me to write to you immediately that Father would like to meet with you for a visit, and this I resolved to do, but I did not have your address and was quite sure that you would not receive the letter.

I wrote to you on Sunday, telling you to arrive in Bordeaux Monday or Tuesday at noon, the hour when they were to arrive.

My letter ended as the other two I had sent before their answer, because I addressed them to Limeuil, so they went to the wrong address.

All this caused great pain and anxiety to our good Mother and all our Mistresses. We owe them a profound gratitude, which, without doubt, we can never show them. We can only pray the Lord to preserve them a long time on earth to continue their apostolate, of which they give us proof every day. They finally left, my dear little sisters, on Friday at 3:00 p.m. Our good Mother wanted me to accompany them, which pleased me very much. The only thing I regretted was not having been able to speak longer with Father.

Lubine is going to Aubenas with Lucie, and Lucia to Nojals, which I suppose did not please Uncle very much, on account of his grandchildren.

I have one more thing to tell you, dearly beloved Father, so gather your strength to listen. Guilbert came to see me, and last Friday he left right away for the hospital; he could no longer stand, and he could breathe only with difficulty and great pain. He told me that he had had chest pains the evening before. Our Mother was in the parlor at that moment and said a few consoling words that did us good.

Finally, dear Papa, we are nailed to the Cross; we should not then complain.

We so outrage Jesus each day that He is obliged to carry a great cross, and He does well to give part of it to those whom He loves. Let us never complain then, but carry our cross with courage and manfully follow the way to Calvary.

This morning I had the great happiness to receive Communion, and I offered to the Divine Saviour all the sufferings He endured for our expiation and [asked] to endure with courage all the afflictions which come to us.

I am happy you are asking to go to the hospital. You will be much better cared for and you will recover more quickly.

Papa, I beg you not to worry too much. We are all well-placed, and you need not be anxious on our account; we are in the hands of God.

Papa, if you can, go to the central office where you told me you had found some letters from home. It seems to me you would find the letters I wrote to you. I have no more to say for the moment but Courage and patience!

Receive, dear Papa, my most tender kisses,

Germaine Castang

Letter 5

Bordeaux, March 27, 1894

My Dear Papa,

You must find the time long in not receiving any news from me. My letter was delayed on account of Holy Week, and today I'm taking advantage of my companion's vacation to write to you. If I did not write to you since New Year's it was because I did not know your address, and then you told me you would come during March.

You told me that you wrote, and I answered all of a sudden without reflection on what I was saying. As for me, after you came to see me, I received no letter from anyone, nor did I write to anyone. You tell me you went on a trip with some people who do nothing but amuse themselves, and it seems to me that all this troubles you. It seems to me, however, that you should be allowed to participate, because it could only bring you some distraction.

Dear Papa, let me tell you my thoughts: you must be bored, but there is a remedy and it is this: you could come here to Bordeaux; you would maybe be happier, and so would I. I will not await a letter from you until your arrival in Bordeaux.

You will tell me where Levy is.

Our Mother is at present a bit fatigued. My excellent Mistresses are for me like mothers who watch over me. I have nothing else to say for the moment as I await the happiness of seeing you and giving you a big hug.

Germaine Castang

P. S. At the moment this letter is going out, I received your second letter. I will read it on my way to the Post Office.

Letter 6

Bordeaux, June 3, 1894

Dearly beloved Sister,

It is nearly six months since I heard from you, and not being able to wait any longer, I send you some news of my dear Papa and of Levy. We are all well, just a little anxious to know if you are perhaps sick as well as Clothilde. For to what should be attributed the long delay of your letter? You must be sick or have too much work, otherwise it would seem you are a bit indifferent. For since my Easter letter, surely you might have found time to answer my last.

It is so sad to be separated from one's family, and you, dear Sister, must understand this, as it has been your experience too. And now you have taken my little sisters and I am quite alone. Only my dear Papa seems to always love me. He came around Easter and stayed for two days in Bordeaux. Like me, he was surprised not to have any news of you.

As for Levy and Guilbert, I don't have much news. I know from dear Papa that Levy's conduct leaves much to be desired.

You must be wondering that I say nothing about going to you. In your last letter you asked me to be more submissive to the will of God. Well, dear Sister, I am entirely resolved to do the Will of our Good God. I have thrown myself into His hands. At present it does not even matter what happens to me, I will repeat with Jesus: FIAT ["Let it be done"]. You must be asking yourself, dearest Sister, where I find this courage and must want me to tell you where I draw it from: it is in the Precious Element with which I am nourished on Sunday.

Ah, yes, dear Sister, you would not believe nor comprehend the joy which animates me when I receive my Jesus! He preserves me from so many little miseries that I continue to be happy.

All my Mistresses are so good to me. Please help me, dearest Sister, to express to them my gratitude by praying to Him who possesses all untarnishable treasures to repay them a hundredfold for their kindness to me.

Give a big hug to my little Clothilde for me. Her Tata Noemi and her Tata Ligori and all her little companions send warmest greetings. My most respectful greetings to Sister St. Herman and to good Sister Anna. Nothing more to tell you for the moment, only [I ask you] to write me a good long letter.

Receive, my dear and beloved Sister, the tender affection and the best kisses of your sister who loves you,

Germaine Castang
Child of Mary

P. S. If you are sending Lucie for the month of August, please have the charity, dearest Sister, to let me know.

Letter 7

Bordeaux, September 22, 1895

Very dear and beloved Sister,

Though my letter is a bit delayed, I hope that in spite of that you will give it a good welcome, for I bring you fresh news of our family.

Let me just ask you: how are you; and my little sisters; are they happy to learn to work or to read? You must give me the details.

I will now tell you of my trip to Nojals. Papa received me a bit coldly at first, following some things which I cannot explain, but in the end he softened.

Madame Mege came to visit me before my departure and begged me to take Levy with me, telling me how much better it would be for him to be around his relatives. I sought him out in order to leave. He remained at our beloved mother's grave; I wanted to go there with all my strength, but it was impossible for me if I could not kneel on that ground so dear to us. I went and left my heart there. I said a fervent prayer as a witness to my passing by.

You know what a variance there is between father and son. I finally convinced our brother to come to make a visit to our father; he was afraid, but does not the Lord receive sinners and the just alike? If he received me, why could he not receive him whom he called his child? So I prepared him for this unexpected visit, and the moment arrived that he had to present himself: a handshake [was given], and there descended some peace upon him [our brother], who stayed a week. He is now at Montastier.

All of our relatives are doing very well. Grandmother

is still sick and Grandfather is still working, since everyone left him.

Suzanne has a little 2-year-old girl and she has lost one.

Angelle has two beautiful little boys. She is no longer at St. Avit Senieur but now stays at Fosse, and Fanelie has very good lodging. At Merle, a little Philomain came to replace Edouard. All this little world was pleased to see me again.

I was also happy to see my Godmother and our cousins. They were all so kind to me. Now, since you are my older sister, let me ask you this question: who is this person who has given you great information about me? I did not think for a moment of remaining in the country. My intention has always been that if I left the convent where I was, it would be with the intention of entering the community.

Your letters about our good Uncle of Nojals gained for me a good scolding, not on the part of Uncle, who is goodness itself, but the pricks which my aunt dealt out by her words at times made me suffer most cruelly. Do not tell anyone. My good Mistresses received me with open arms, and I threw myself into them as into those of her who once used to open them to me also.

Until now I have lived in hope, but I am beginning to lose it completely. I intend to write to our Reverend Mother: this is my secret. Since my dear Mistresses said they would not receive me unless I were completely healed, I have renounced all hope, and for two or three days my tears flow in the absence of my dear Papa. It is hard for me to pronounce the *fiat* of resignation. Pray, dear Sister, as I in my turn prayed for you and offered my small mortifications which I performed throughout the day.

I enclose the letter of our brother Guilbert which I received yesterday. An affectionate hello to my Sister Anna and Sister Theodore. My deepest thanks to your good Reverend Mother, and I'd like to offer her this image from me. I slipped and said "ours," but as I do not think I will ever be able to say that, I corrected myself.

I embrace you heartily as well as my dear little angels, from whom I would never have been separated if . . . [the rest is illegible].

Letter 8

Bordeaux, November 1, 1895

Good and very dear Papa,

After my departure I often thought of you, and especially of the anxiety which worried you the last days I passed in your company.

If I have not written yet, the cause was that I was waiting for news of Guilbert to send to you.

Now, let me ask you how your health is. Do not allow yourself to suffer too much from the cold. Dear Papa, you must have found me a bit distant during this vacation. Forgive me, I took so much pleasure in seeing all our other relatives that at times I may have hurt you. Do not think for this that my affection for you has lessened, it does nothing but grow with each passing day. If I did not stay with you it is because I would no longer have the same life as here, and that if your health were worse, you have my address. In your solitude it appears to me your days must seem very long, and so to interrupt for a moment the silence which reigns in the little dwelling which you inhabit, I allow myself to write you a long letter, which I hope will please you more than the mewing of your little cat. Guilbert is at Tananarive and suffers much from hunger or other miseries. On his return you will doubtless receive a visit from him. I hope that your heart will be open to receive him, for, after so much suffering, it seems most natural to make one forget all the pains by lavishing affection.

You will have the charity to give me news of Levy.

Tomorrow is Holy Souls day, and my heart is saddened as my thoughts are carried to the dear remains of our beloved dead; but I am consoled in praying for them, for that is my only hope.

In the same spirit of prayer, tomorrow, dear Papa, please, while giving the better part to my dear mother and brother, have an intention for me and for Sr. St. Valentin, whom, I gathered on my return, has died. Please send me news of the Sisters of Nojals if you have any.

My tongue has no more to say, but my heart knows how to defend you on every occasion and puts these words on my lips: I love you very much, dear Papa, and to give you proof, I embrace you a thousand times.

Germaine Castang

P. S. Your traveling bag is waiting. If some happy chance would allow you to come, don't miss that chance.

Letter 9 (2 letters in one envelope)

Bordeaux, December 8, 1895

Dearly beloved Sister,

At last the day has arrived that I can write to you. With impatience I have waited to send you my best wishes for your feast day and the New Year. It is with all my heart that I say to you, Happy Feastday! and as a gift I offer my prayers. You will tell me I am a bit early with the New Year; well, all the better—I shall be the first to greet my eldest sister!

They are always the same, beloved Sister, the wishes I form in your regard. It is always from the depths of my heart that I say to the Divine Infant of the Creche: "You know the needs of a big sister, and that she is the guardian of my two dear little sisters. Great gifts are in your little hands; give to my sister all that You know she needs, supply for me who am so far away and would like so much to give her a big kiss." I have some things to tell you, but on a feast day they would certainly sadden you. No, I will rest content to tell you only how much and how great is my pain in worrying about our dear Papa. He must, without doubt, be displeased with me. I wrote to him but I got no answer. What will become of me if I no longer have anyone— no sister, no father, no brother: it is too much. You are much better off, for you have the little ones.

News of Guilbert is not very reassuring, for I have heard nothing since I wrote you last. Levy is not in the country, he deceived me in telling me he would come. You will be so kind as to offer my best wishes for the New Year to Sr. Theodore and Sr. Anna. I quickly end my letter so that I can add a little something for my little sisters. Receive, dear Sister, with my New Year's wishes . . . [manuscript unfinished]

My dear little Sisters,

Do you think, my darlings, that I have forgotten you? No, certainly not! Chase away such thoughts, for each time I write to our big sister I ask about you.

You must have grown very much since your departure, and I hope that you are growing also very wise.

You will say that I am a bit proud; nevertheless, let me tell you what I think: you must be a little more knowledgeable than I, but do not go mocking me if I make [grammatical] mistakes all along; I am only too happy you are getting a good education.

My dear little Lucia, it is your birthday too. I give you a real big hug, and for the moment that is all I can do, but let us hope that the Christ Child will fill my purse at Christmas, and then I will send gifts to my dear little sisters for the New Year. And my little Clothilde? Is she in good health? Is she quite happy and does she pray often to the dear little Jesus? That is all I ask for her, and that she never annoy her Mistresses. You know how soon God took our darling mother from us; well, your Mistresses are in her place, so try always to please them by your conduct.

I should so like to have a little letter from the two of you. Give my New Year's wishes to Sr. Didier and ask her to let you write.

Be always good and loving to our older sister, who is so good to you.

Pray that you may always be very good little girls, and pray for me who needs your prayers.

My dear little sisters, I embrace you heartily,

Germaine Castang

I beg my dear sister to give this letter to Lucia and Clothilde.

Letter 10

(Note: This letter, although it is dated April 3, 1896, must surely follow the next one, dated April 12. It is evident for several reasons that there is an error of date.)

Bordeaux, April 3, 1896

Good and dearest Papa,

You desired so much my picture; well, here it is. It was taken of me clothed as one of the boarders with my Child of Mary ribbon—which looks white, but it is blue. Now that I have fulfilled my promise, you also have made one, and will give me your consent [to enter the convent]. I therefore wait impatiently this week, so that I can send everything in next Sunday.

I shall hope that you will write me also a nice, long letter; that will please me very much, because it makes me happy when I feel close to you.

I was told that they wrote to you to get permission for me to stay a little longer with you. I am sorry, but I told myself: Here is my first sacrifice.

I received a letter from my dear Lucie, who, far from blaming me, has encouraged me to enter [the Poor Clares] this way, which leads to true happiness.

I sent the list that they gave me for my trousseau to my Uncle. He still has not responded.

What more can I say to you, good and dearest Papa? So many things my heart does find and always will! Yes, Papa, my heart bleeds to think that our separation is to be prolonged, but I have heard it well said, at times, that life is ephemeral; that the days here below are short in comparison to those of eternity. I have understood this, Papa; know that it is for this I leave you, with all that is dear to me in this world, to think of nothing but our reunion one day in Heaven.

Guilbert did not write; I would not be surprised if he is even sicker. Kindly give my news to our cousin Clemence, as well as to his daughter, whose name I have forgotten, and say a few nice things for me.

I went to see my new Superiors last Sunday; they await your consent, as I do. Try then, dear Papa, not to make me wait. Every day my heart pounds until I see your letter.

Receive, dear Papa, with the assurance of my constant affection, my tenderest kisses,

Germaine Castang

Letter 11

Bordeaux, April 12, 1896

Very dear and beloved Sister,

Have you been expecting my letter? Perhaps I have been forestalled, but I can explain matters better than anyone else.

On Easter Monday, while my companions were on vacation, Sister Noemi, always disposed to give pleasure, allowed me to go out on a walk with one of our assistant Mistresses. Toward the end of our walk we went to the Poor Clares to call on one of the religious we knew. Without thinking at all of my vocation, I began to say how happy those good nuns must be and that I would never have such happiness. This good Sister asked me if I wanted to speak to the Mother Abbess and explain to her my situation. I couldn't count on myself at all for something which to me seemed truly insurmountable. But it was the Lord Himself who guided me and prepared the way for me.

The enclosure curtains of the grille were drawn for me, which allowed me to see four kind Mothers who had goodness painted all over their faces! In any other circumstance I would have felt myself blushing, but no, one would have thought that I had passed my life with them. They questioned me much about you and all the family. The Reverend Mother Vivaire pleaded my cause with Reverend Mother Abbess. They finally left me, telling me to pray and hope.

Is this not the realization of all my dreams? I was almost overcome with happiness, but there is still more. On Wednesday morning, Mother St. Pierre received a note announcing that I had been received and asking me to go to them on the next Sunday. To my great amazement, our good Mother saw how God calls souls and uses everything to lead them to Himself.

She came to announce this good news to me and told me to write to Papa, and that is what I did immediately. While waiting for the answer, I went on Sunday to the Poor Clares, where they again opened the grille to me, but this time there were many of the Sisters. Among them they pointed out one who entered at 15 and is now 18, and that she will be my "good angel." They talked to me a long time and decided that if there were no impediments, they would receive me on the feast of Our Lady of Good Counsel. They made an exception for me; I even showed them my leg.

Only Papa's permission is still required, and he says that he will do what you advise. My dearest Sister, if you truly love me and have understood my heart's past sufferings, examine these things and admire the ways of Providence. My first desire was the contemplative life, the life of the Sisters of St. Clare. When I was but 15, at the sight of the monastery I received an impression that I should never be able to explain, and yet I was refused.

Then I resolved to go wherever—it mattered not. Last year at the time of the retreat, I decided to enter whatever community I could, and I received a second refusal. God was waiting for me at this hour, and it is the Poor Clares who want me. I rejoice, and all my Mistresses rejoice with me; my confessor also is in admiration of God's design for me.

Dearest Sister, you must not be selfish, and especially you must not grieve, but be glad with me. Consider that you do not want me to live at home with my dear Papa, nor do I wish to stay on here—it is not my element. Furthermore, you know that for a long time now I've nourished this desire in my heart, and I am not entering impulsively or without reflection. Oh, if only you knew how happy they all seem! Besides, there is a novitiate of one year; all I ask is to be allowed to try. Do then, dearest Sister, help me with Papa. I am leaving all, but I will find all things. I know well the miseries of life in the world and the trials of the convent; as long as we are going to God, we may as well give ourselves entirely. You need not fear for me, there's only a six-month postulancy, and I won't be allowed to fast until I'm 21. One goes barefoot—so? I feel just as cold with thick woolen stockings on as with none! I have only had broken chilblains once, when I walked too much at the time of our dear mother's death. If it is God's Will, I shall succeed. You know I shall sometimes be able to write, and one can see relatives two or three times a year. My dear Sister, I have always helped you, now you must help me. Make Papa see that true happiness is not to be found in this world, but one may have it by belonging entirely to Jesus without reserve. Have you yourself not told me many times that it is not we who choose but God who chooses us? I have been chosen, so rejoice with me!

Two words about my poor Guilbert. He is here in Bordeaux since Friday evening, sick with a high fever which won't go down. He suffered much from hunger and thirst and many other privations. He still has seven more months of service and left for Rochefort today. He should have gone to recover in the country, but he wrote to Papa without getting an answer. I will write more on the subject in my next letter. Before leaving you I want to tell you to give a big hug to my little sisters and thank them for their nice letters.

Your sister who loves you and will love you unto the last day!

G. Castang

Letter 12 (3 letters in one envelope)

Bordeaux, May 16, 1896

Dearly beloved Sister,

I think that you will be surprised to see that I [i.e., my photo] arrive before the letter! From now on I will stay with you. You are not happy about this, but it gives me great pleasure to live under the same roof as you, dear Sister, and my little darlings. I would like for you to come with me also in this way, but I know that what I am asking is an impossibility. So, finally you have my portrait. In looking at me you can well say: "This is my sister"; in fact, it is me, exactly as I am. Here is my boarding school dress. The Child of Mary ribbon looks white, but it is blue.

Look at me well, dear Sister, and you will see me anxiously seeking for the reason I [here the original text is illegible].

But no, that is not possible. I cannot believe it. I will not allow myself to stop.

Oh, here is the last of my letters, and I beg you immediately not to allow me to imagine things that cannot be! Do not be mysterious any longer; tell me what is happening. How many times you have said to me: "Tell me your pains, which are mine also." Well, now if it is I who say that, why do you hide something from me? Am I a stranger to you? Have I given you some pain? Oh no, dear Sister, speak, I beg you! I do not have a big heart, as I am a creature, but you are my sister, and on that account my heart is enlarged for you. Nothing will surprise me anymore, for I have understood many things, and they only serve to detach me more and more from the things here below.

You will be happy to know that I am soon to enter the Poor Clares. My entrance date is fixed for June 12, Feast of the Sacred Heart. On this blessed day, keep me in your prayers, dearest Sister. As for me, I place myself entirely in the Sacred Heart of Jesus. All my desires are being satisfied: a brother restored to my tenderness and the religious life to which I aspired so ardently. I truly possess the fullness of joy.

You have saddened me by your last letter, but again,

I cannot believe what I think. Please clarify this mystery in your next letter.

Papa sent me his consent this week. Guilbert is in the military hospital of Rochefort. I have no news of him nor of Levy, whom I have not seen since last year.

My Uncle has been so good to me: he sent me the money I need for the religious garb—130 francs—not to mention the dowry.

Before the page ends I must address a little note to my dear little sisters. Oh, what it costs me, dearest Sister, to leave you without knowing when I will have the happiness of writing or seeing you again! I dare not say: Never, for my heart says: Hope. If not here below, at least there above: this is the sacrifice I make to Jesus in giving myself to Him.

My Sister a thousand times dear, receive the big kisses of a sister who loves you with all her heart and who will always think of you.

Here is my new address:

> Very Reverend Mother Abbess
> Monastery of the Ave Maria
> Rue de Clarisses
> Talence—Bordeaux Gironde

Write me as soon as you can. I am sending you a stamp. The Sisters of Nojals have my rosary and my First Communion medals, which they will send on to you. I spent about eight days in the country and saw everyone. They were quite happy. It was impossible for me to visit our beloved Mother's grave, another sacrifice which cost me much.

My dear little Goddaughter,

You will weep, my little Lucia, when you learn that your Godmother is going to enter the convent, and that perhaps you will never see her again. You had good reason in saying to me that possibly we would never meet again. That is true, my darling; nevertheless, I have the hope that if you cannot come to see me, we will meet one day in Heaven. Isn't that the great reunion we await? I will pray for you, my dearest one, that you may grow in wisdom and that you will make yourself worthy of the favors that are in store for you.

Farewell to my little Lucia, I embrace you tightly,

Germaine Castang

My dear little Lubine,

You are the last, but not the least. I did not forget you, nor will I forget you when I enter the Poor Clares. I will pray that you will be an example to your little sister Lucia, and that you always be the joy of your Mistresses. You must be my messenger to offer them my most respectful greetings. I have nothing to give to you; our big sister, Sr. St. Germain, will give you my photo. Farewell, my little Lubinette. Though in body I am far away, I am very near you in my thoughts and I embrace you a thousand times.

Letter 13

(Note: This letter is actually of July 20, 1896 because Sr. Eleonore of St. Joseph, the novice mentioned in the letter, took the habit on July 19, 1896.)

Bordeaux, June 20, 1896

Praised be Jesus Christ

Good and dearest Papa,

You must think that I am indifferent toward you, but you will forgive me if I tell you why it seems that way.

Yesterday, Sunday, we had a truly wonderful feast. There was a Clothing ceremony, and since I am the only postulant left, the good Mothers allowed me to participate. I was all dressed in white the whole day, and I do not need to tell you, for you can imagine, that I was not in the least unhappy. You were not mistaken in what you told me before leaving.

They love me here as at Nazareth; you can be at peace. I have no mother any longer, but here I have found some who are just as good. I remained five years in the workroom with Sr. Noemi, who was so kind to me.

Well, I can say that my heart has never attached itself anywhere as it has to this house in the month that I have lived here!

It is true that I so desired to be a religious—and to see my wishes fulfilled is for me a great joy.

I have some Sisters who show me such kind attentions. They look for everything that could please me. In a word, dearest Papa, I do not deserve to have such good Superiors and Sisters.

Mr. de Bladbourg sent me a paper stating that you

are in very good health and that you were so good as to send us some cherries.

Our Superiors were very touched by this kindness— so much so that all the Sisters begged me to thank you and assure you of their prayers.

In your last letter you told me you were so curious, and so I will tell you all that I can to satisfy you.

I am sure you will be happy if I tell you the name of our Reverend Mother Abbess, so here it is: Claire Isabelle of St. Francis of Assisi, as well as that of our dear Mother Vicaress, which I have already told you, but in case you have forgotten, it is Seraphine of the Heart of Jesus. They are such pretty names, and those of my Sisters are all just as beautiful.

You mentioned that when your vineyard yields, you will make us a present of some barrels of wine. I look forward to that, as the monastery casks are not over-flowing!

You can be sure that at the Monastery of the Ave Maria all is received with gratitude. You were anxious to know if they would be accepted. Well, let this answer reassure you.

I had occasion to send a little note to my dear little sisters, as well as to Lucie. I have not received any news and don't know if she's fallen ill. If you have word, please let me know.

I'm still rejoicing over yesterday's celebration, which gave me hope. I thought to myself: "In five months it will be my turn." I need not give you the details, for you know already.

I was hoping a letter would accompany the basket, but since you did not give me that pleasure, I hope you will [write] now that I have told you so many nice things.

Good and dearest Papa, receive the sentiments of affection of one who will never forget you.

Sister Lucia

Letter 14

J.M.J.

Bordeaux, June 21, 1896

Good and dearest Papa,

You must await with impatience one of my letters. Well then, here is one which brings good and excellent news of your little Germaine.

She is already acclimated to the Monastery of the Ave Maria—so much so that she has not been bored one single instant.

One must not believe all that is said about cloistered communities. I have nothing to complain of. If all the poor were like me, there would no longer be any. They do not let me die of hunger here.

We seek happiness here on earth and find it not. For me, dear Papa, I need not look far. I have found it here, far from the dangers of the world, beneath the loving eyes of Jesus. We all want to go to Him in Heaven, and so that all the family be led there, it is far better that I sacrifice the happiness of seeing you here on earth and that we all be reunited in Heaven. Last night I rose for Matins [early morning prayer] for the first time. So often I was slow in getting out of bed, but now I am quick. It is without a doubt the good God who lavishes His graces upon me, and I beg Him for a favor for my dear Papa. He knows the graces of which you are in need; and besides, you have made some sacrifices, and the good Lord will not leave them without recompense.

I left good Mother St. Pierre, who told me that although I was leaving her, I'd always be her child. I felt keenly this mark of affection on her part. I left my first Mother to find other, even better ones, who take pains to direct me in the way of Truth.

I will tell you quite frankly, dear Papa, that my heart sighs when I think of you and of my good Mistresses of Nojals and Bordeaux. It is a sacrifice which I offer every day to Our Lord, but for the rest I am very happy to have left all.

When I receive your news, would you tell me about Lucie? It is a long time since I've received anything from her.

I have other things to tell you, dearest Papa, but I shall keep them for next time. So I close by assuring you that the farther apart we are, the more and the greater the affection I have for you.

Germaine Castang

Letter 15

God Alone †

St. Clare of the Ave Maria of Talence, November 17, 1896

Praised be Jesus Christ! Hail Mary!

Very dear and beloved Sister,

Truly I have a great mind to be angry: your reproaches are unmerited.

You tell me that my letters are rare. I do not understand that. Our good Mothers were so kind as to allow me to respond right away, and I wrote you a four-page letter.

Since you do not receive my letters, it is not worth it to write you a long one. I have many things to tell you, but I'll just tell you the reason I am writing to you. If you receive my letter, you will answer me and I will tell you the rest.

Our dear Mothers have chosen next Saturday as my Clothing day.

I cannot tell you my joy. I recommend myself to your prayers and ask you to offer Holy Communion for me.

Dearest Sister, you will think that my letter is too short. It hurts me to write so little. But I am obligated now. It pains me not to share my feelings with you as in the past, if you do not profit by them.

The sister of our beloved Mother was in Aubenas when you were on retreat, having come to Bordeaux shortly before that. I had the pleasure of seeing her.

She had the charity to go out of her way to bring you my news, but they refused to allow you to see her, as well as my little sisters, for whom she went out of her way twice but met always the same refusal. I was really vexed at all that, but it was not your fault, and it pained me to make you suffer the consequences.

Farewell, therefore, dearly beloved Sister, I love you always in the Hearts of Jesus and Mary.

Sister Lucia

P. S. You will certainly look for a holy picture to send me. Spare yourself the trouble, it would only encumber me. A Poor Clare should possess nothing. Accept that which I send you, and the other two are for our little sisters.

Letter 16

God Alone †

St. Clare of the Ave Maria of Talence, December 29, 1896

I have chosen the better part, and it shall not be taken from me.

Dearest Papa,

I am happy that the first of the year is approaching, that I may offer you my best wishes for a good year crowned with success, good health, and not too much suffering down there all alone. Finally, you have told me that you are never bored, and that reassures me.

You have left me a long time without any news of you. I hope that soon you will give me this pleasure.

As for me, I cough a little, but our Reverend Mothers take good care of me—if only you knew! I do not know how to show them my gratitude.

Guilbert came to see me. He did not leave for Madagascar. He is completely cured and now is staying permanently at Saintes.

Good and dearest Papa, receive the prayers and New Year's wishes of her who loves you always.

Sr. Celine of the Presentation

Letters of Sister Marie de St. Germain (Lucie Castang) to her Younger Sister, Sister Marie Celine (Germaine Castang)

Letter 1

J.M.J.

Urcel, August 21, 1896

My very dear and beloved Germaine,

Here I am, so late in responding to your last letter; my silence must have caused you pain, and I myself suffer in making you wait so long. You must not think it is negligence, and even less, indifference. You know well my love for you, my joy in your entrance into religion; you must know it still. None of these reasons has been the cause of my prolonged silence; rather it is due to a combination of circumstances which would be too long to recount and would serve only to distract you.

Ah, if you had as [little a] taste for teaching, my dear Sister, as I do, after six years a retreat would indeed seem sweet to you! You know it is hard for us to form the hearts of these young girls in virtue nowadays, when everything conspires to pervert them, and when the teachings and example of the school are paralyzed by those of the family.

Discouragement threatens to overcome me. I can assure you that I ask myself what excuse I can make hold up before God when He demands of me an account for these children which He has confided to me.

Oh yes, you are quite happy—or rather, you are all quite happy, my Sisters, behind your grilles—I believe without a doubt that you taste such happiness! Yes, my dear Germaine, I have told you already, I have hoped for your happiness for over four years now; I have longed for it and I did not tell you. But if today I raise the veil on the subject, it is not so that you may speak of it to our dear Papa or to Uncle or even to Sister du St. Sacrément. That which I reveal to you I still keep hidden from them; I do not even have enough courage to speak of it to our Reverend Mother, though she is so good.

I beg you, my dearly beloved, pray for me, I have need of it. I do not want to give in to a temptation, and that is what I am afraid of.

You told me your Reverend Mother is so good. Well then, do beg her for a little remembrance for me; I shall not forget her. You can count on me, but I also count on you.

I saw our dear little sisters yesterday. They were radiant to see me, and my joy was no less, as you can imagine. I read with real pleasure the letter which you wrote to them. It will not be long before you receive an answer from them. And the news of the family, particularly of Guilbert, interested me.

I forgot to tell you that I assisted at a Clothing ceremony on July 7 at the monastery of Poor Clare Nuns of Vals, half an hour from Urcel. I was vividly impressed—but even more, I envied the lot of the young lady who, saying an eternal farewell to the world, consecrated herself body and soul to the service of the good God. The Reverend Mother Abbess with whom we had the happiness to speak seemed to me of such goodness. Oh, my Sister, how blessed you are to be far from the tumult of the world, far from the occasions of offending God.

Two months ago, Sr. Theodore was moved; presently I am with Sr. Stephana, who for me is of unparalleled kindness.

I do not expect an answer to this letter; you will, nevertheless, give me this pleasure. If it is your intention, do not delay in writing. We leave on the 29th for our retreat. Think of me, if you will.

Your Sister who loves you tenderly

P. S. Thank you, my good little Sister, for having sent me your photograph. You could not have given me a greater happiness. In my moments of sadness I console myself by you, but you don't answer me, and I would love so much to chat with you verbally.

Letter 2

J.M.J.

Privas, January 24, 1897

My very dear Sr. Celine of the Presentation,

I expressed my astonishment to our dear Papa at not having received from you any answer to the last letter I wrote after your Clothing. To appease me, he sent me your New Year's letter: a truly excellent idea, in which I delighted. Thanks to him I know you were named Sr. Celine of the Presentation: this is a magnificent name, very much to my liking. I love to believe that your new Patroness, all powerful in the sight of God, will watch over you and accord you the grace to become a worthy daughter of St. Clare.

All that you told me about the goodness of your Reverend Mother Abbess moves me very much. Please have the charity to thank her for me and recommend me to her fervent prayers. I do not doubt yours, because you know my great need of them.

Around New Year's I received some letters from many of our relatives. Our Uncle was the first, poor dear Uncle. How good he is, and how he loves us! Let us love him well in return and pray for him and his family. His son, our cousin Joseph, has not written yet, but I know his rheumatism is getting better. Aunt Suzanne was not late this year. Her letter is charming—I wish I could send it to you. She asked me to offer you her best wishes for 1897: they're already a bit outdated, what do you think? As for Aunt Angele, she never makes the effort to give me news of her family, nor does Eloi give news of our dear grandparents. Let us think of them before God in this world and hope to see them again in Heaven—for here below, we must rest content with keeping them in our hearts.

I should like to speak to you of our little sisters, but I have not heard from them in a long time. However, they must have written to you because I sent them your address.

Lubine is preparing to make her First Communion and Lucia is learning her catechism in preparation. I read the few details you gave me about Guilbert, but they're not enough; I would like to write to him. Please give me his address, and that of Levy also. They are really indifferent toward me to let the first of the year go by without writing me a letter.

Our dear Papa is always into his business up to his neck: it is a need for him. Let us always love him and pray the good God never to abandon him. By the way, I forgot to tell you that he does not have time to answer your New Year's letter and he asked me to tell you. Like you, he has caught a cold, but it's passing. I myself just got over a kind of head and chest cold.

But what do you expect? We must pay tribute to the winter, and it is not very mild here in Privas. The snow covers the mountains, the roofs of houses, the branches of the trees—and I can assure you that no one is anxious to stick our nose in the wind! You will think me a blabber, and perhaps you are right, but I'm finished. I've come to the end of the page, and besides, it is time to go to Vespers [evening prayer], where I have my "rendezvous" with all those whom I love.

Your devoted,

Sr. St. Germain

PART FOUR

Graces and Favors

Attributed to the Intercession of Sister Marie Celine

Graces and Favors

Milwaukee
November 7, 1924

I am asked to send you an alms in thanksgiving for a *great favor* granted by Sister Marie Celine. My friend has been always subject to fits, but since invoking the aid of Sister Celine and wearing her relic, she has not had one, and trusts now that she is permanently cured. She is so thankful to God and grateful to Sister Celine for her help and intercession in her regard. I have already circulated the books and pictures you so kindly sent to me, and the people here as well as the children are very much attracted by this little Saint of Our Blessed Lord.   —Rev. X

Milwaukee
November 19, 1924

Dear Reverend Mother,

I wish to notify you that I have received *great favors* through the intercession of Sister Marie Celine of the Presentation. I was in very bad health and had recourse to her, praying her intercession in my regard, that if it were God's will I might be restored to complete health of body. You will be delighted to know that my prayer was heard and answered. She has also granted to me my heart's desire. She has opened the Convent gates for me, and I am now ready and waiting to enter the Sisterhood, which I have always desired.

I am so grateful to your holy novice.   —X

New Orleans, U.S.A.
January 11, 1925

Dear Rev. Mother,

I feel that I must write and tell you of a *wonderful answer* to prayer that I have had through the intercession of your dear Sister, Marie Celine of the Presentation. My son had given up the Faith, and for four long years refused to have anything to do with it. Great was my grief and many the prayer I sent up for his conversion. But it all seemed of no avail. Hearing of Sister Celine, I at once had recourse to her, and I promised her that if she would get this great favor, so pleasing to God, for me, that I would acknowledge it to the Mother House in her honor. Great was my joy when I found that my prayer *had been heard* and was beginning to be answered. My son began to look towards Holy Church once again, and on Christmas morning attended his duties, receiving Holy Communion. He declares that he is now very happy, and has great peace of heart and mind. I feel *absolutely confident* that Sister Marie Celine obtained *this favor* for me from the Sacred Heart of Our Divine Lord through Our Lady of Perpetual Succor.

Oh how grateful I am to God for His great mercy! and to Sister Celine for her help!

I remain, dear Mother, yours.   —Mrs. E.L.

For the past two months the sister of Miss C.Z.H. has had a nervous breakdown due to overwork. Her condition has affected her mind, so that she is in a delirium most of the time, and suffers from thoughts circling so fast as to make her head throb. It is a most pitiful sight, says the sister, and the doctors say they cannot do anything for her. So the sister trusts in the Heavenly Physician. After a Novena made by a community of Poor Clares, she rallied, almost miraculously, long enough to be prepared to receive the Last Sacraments. But her normal condition lasted a day or so when she relapsed and did not improve, in fact, she became weaker physically as well. The kind, heartbroken sister, who already had received a *favor* through the intercession of Sister Marie Celine, decided to ask our prayers for the recovery of Miss X's mind and rapid restoration of her former good health. She sent an alms toward the expenses of Sister Marie Celine's Beatifiction, and promised more if Miss X was restored to her normal health.

(From a letter of Miss C.Z.H.—September)

The Sequel

October 19, 1925

I am pleased to advise you that my sister M. has recovered her mind fully and is normal, as far as I can notice, in everything she says and does. I am very grateful and will ever give thanks.   —C.H.

Cleveland, Ohio
October 18, 1925

I presented a relic and a picture with the prayer for
Beatification of Sister Marie Celine to Sophie Sosnowska.
She had been ill for five years and could not walk. Her
mother had been doctoring her little girl for many years.
The doctors told her the girl had tuberculosis of the
bones, and that there was no cure for her. Two weeks
ago the mother told me the doctors were surprised to
see Sophie improving, as they claimed there was no cure
for her. When I first approached Sophie she was like
one numb, could not walk nor move her body, or swing
her hands. But if you could see her now. She is improving rapidly. Sophie is only 13 years of age, and said if
she is going to be really well, she will become a Nun.
She is very happy. . . .   —Miss Josephine Sygment

Greengate, London, E.13
March 26, 1926

This is a letter in *thanksgiving* to Sister Marie Celine.
My mother is a widow, and my brother, who is her
chief support, was out of work for a long time, which
was a cause of great anxiety to her. I said a Hail Mary
each day to your little Sister Celine, promising, should
she obtain from Our Divine Lord a position for him in
business, I would make known this *favor.* My brother
is now at work with a promise of future success.

—D.B.

Mrs. J.Mc.N., Co. Antrim, writes to Giovanni Ser-pentelli under date April 22nd: "I made a Novena to Sister Marie Celine to ask her to pray for the cure of my aunt's leg. She had been suffering from an ulcer-ated leg for twenty years, and the doctors had advised her to have the leg taken off. So I made a Novena to Sister Marie Celine, and now her leg is completely cured."

The following tribute comes from a Nurse Matron: "May 17th, 1926. In the month of March of this year a patient was brought in to me suffering from scar-latina and diphtheria (a mixture of diseases). The patient (a child of two years) was very ill, and the doc-tor had little hope for its recovery, as the infection had gone into the eye and its appearance was very bad. However, the father of the child (who is a very reli-gious man) had faith and great devotion to Sister Marie Celine, so he asked me to apply her relic to the child. I did so, and the child began to improve and was a perfect cure.

I kept the relic in my possession, and some time after the above occurrence a child was brought in to me suffering from cellulitis. The doctor made several incisions and the wound didn't even bleed, it was so bad. The trouble was all in the head. It was an awful sight. The doctor told me to bandage it up anyway; that the child was dying and he could do nothing for it. I acquainted the friends and told them there was no hope, that it was impossible to cure cellulitis in the head. At the same time I produced the relic of Sister Marie Celine and applied it to the head of the child. The next day the doctor was surprised to see the child alive, and so improved. It continued to improve every day, and we sent it home a complete cure.

We have great devotion to Sister Marie Celine. We call her 'our Saint'; and we are sure she will keep a kindly eye over us and help us in our critical work here."

A Dublin woman says: "A little girl here had a lump on her gums, caused by bad teeth. Her mouth was in such a state that the dentist would not make an extraction. She could barely open her mouth. She suffered intense agony. She applied the relic of Marie Celine to her jaw and obtained immediate relief. Now she is quite better."

Tubize
March 4, 1907

It has been so consoling for me to learn that you have taken to heart the Novena that I asked for last week.

During the time that I was writing to you my mother suffered very much. Confident that your prayers presented to the Good God by your dear Marie Celine would be heard, I made an intention, saying: "Dear Marie Celine, in order to show that you are going to help us, please obtain for Mama immediate relief."

This was said about ten o'clock in the morning. Mama had another bad turn after that, then towards noon she went to sleep and slept till about half-past three. On awakening she did not feel the least pain. Nevertheless she did not dare move, as she was afraid that the least movement might cause her pains to come back again. However they had so entirely disappeared, that the following day she was able to come down-stairs.

Since then she has not had the least pain. She has entirely removed, and has resumed again all the duties of her daily life   —Georgette Vandenborre

Soulac-sur-Mer (Gironde)
August 21, 1907

On Friday I was suddenly attacked with neuritis, accompanied by dreadful pains, which for twenty-four hours did not allow me one minute's respite. I said to myself, "The disease has conquered." Covered with per-spiration, and not able to rest either lying down or on foot, I was wondering what I should do. As I was not able to remain longer seated, I arose, and found myself *suddenly* and *completely* restored to health, whereas usually these attacks disappear gradually and gener-ally take from eight to fifteen days to disappear alto-gether.

At the very moment of my cure a relative, who hap-pened to be visiting me, thought of Sister Celine, and implored Heaven through her intercession by reciting a *Pater* and *Ave* that I might get a little rest.

So, Mother Superior, you can add this favor to the list of those already obtained through the intercession of Sister Marie Celine, and I beg you to accept my most respectful greetings.   —Ferdinand Rosier

Versoix, Canton de Geneva, Switzerland
September 25, 1907

After having the pleasure of reading the Life of your dear Sister Marie Celine, I prayed through her intercession for the cure of my young sister, who had been grievously ill for eight months.

I am firmly convinced that it is owing to the Novena that we made through the intercession of Sister Celine, that she is now completely restored to health. Also I wish to keep my promise by informing you of this cure, which has been *truly miraculous.*

I have very great confidence in Marie Celine. Would you kindly do me the favor of sending me some sachets of her clothing?   —Madame Tronchet

Saint-Vincent-Jalmoutiers
October 17, 1907

I am happy to be able to tell you that, thanks to the intervention of Sister Marie Celine, I have just been cured of a great infirmity.

From my infancy I had always suffered in my left knee. Sometimes my knee would get so stiff that I could not walk for several days. My family did not pay much attention to it until I had reached the age of fifteen years; from that time I was not able to walk at all. Mamma consulted several doctors, who told her that all they could do would be to give me some relief, but that it would be impossible to cure me. They said that I had arthritis, and that it would be necessary to use an electric needle and to put my leg in a cast. After much care and a long rest I was able to walk again, but I had always to wear my knee-piece and bands. Moreover it was necessary for me to have my knee pierced with the electric needle regularly every three or four months.

In 1905 I was an assistant-governess in an institution at Plantin, near Paris. I was not able to finish the year on account of my knee, which in July held me up completely. I was deeply grieved, and suffered very much.

This year in the month of June I went to Bordeaux, where one of my friends took me to the tomb of Sister Marie Celine. There I prayed with fervor, but without thinking of asking for the cure of my knee. It was only on my return that Madame Guvingnan made me more acquainted with Celine. She also gave me a sachet containing a particle of the clothing of Marie Celine, which I have not ceased to wear.

Immediately I laid aside my knee-piece and bands and began a Novena. I promised Sister Marie Celine to be grateful to her all my life and to give her my First Communion Crown. From that moment I have had *no more pain*. I have gone for long walks without the least fatigue, and I am able to kneel down, a thing I was not able to do before.

I am very grateful to Sister Marie Celine. I am under her protection, and I shall make her known to all those who need her assistance. —M. Fayiut

Poiters, January 9, 1909

. . . We are very fond of our dear little Sister Marie Celine—she has obtained many *graces* for us.

I told you that we had been to her tomb during the month of September. While there I prayed only for spiritual intentions, and my husband did likewise; but on leaving the cemetery he felt impelled to ask for the cure of his sciatica which had been troubling him for a long time, and from which he was suffering very much at the moment. Immediately he felt a cold sensation passing through his whole body, and the *disease disappeared.*

Reverend Mother Seraphine by writing this book has certainly accomplished a work that must be pleasing to the Good God, as her book will be the means of helping many to sanctify their souls.   —L. Thiolier

Cette
September 25, 1908

My love and thanks to Sister Celine for having cured my daughter! She had an attack of influenza, and was consumed by fever for a period of three months and a half, but *the fever abated* as soon as I placed on her neck a piece of linen worn by Sister Celine, and her cure began from that moment. Praise, glory and thanksgiving be to Sister Marie Celine!   —Mme. Masse

P. S. The little miraculous relic was lent to me by one of my friends, who is expecting to soon receive *"A Lily of the Cloister."* As she has asked for several copies, I have requested her to put one aside for me, as I am anxious to read the Life of one who is so dear to us. If you are able at the same time to send her another relic, I would be pleased to have one in order to be able to render service to my neighbors.

Madrid, Calle Velasquez, 10
May 28, 1909

A.M.D.G.,

. . . One of our Sisters had a very serious attack of erysipelas on the face and scalp. The doctor was very much worried, as he feared brain-fever. While I was beginning to use the remedies prescribed by the doctor, I conceived the idea of putting a sachet of Marie Celine on her head. This had scarcely been done when the pains, which had been so terrible, *ceased.* This disease which had at first appeared so serious no longer caused any anxiety, and at the end of seven days our Sister was able to get up and leave her cell.

For our Mother,

Sister Marie, of Saint Irénée
Religious of Marie-Thérèse

Montpellier
September 22, 1909

What emotions I feel in beginning this letter! When
I think that it is to Marie Celine's Superior that I am
writing, it seems as if my letter were going to herself.
Everybody here loves dear Marie Celine, who has just
obtained for us *a miraculous cure.*

Following an excitement, a swelling appeared under-
neath my father's chin, and it so increased in size that
it spread behind his ear. It was twenty centimeters in
length and as hard as a stone. After seeing several
doctors in Cette, my native place, we consulted those
of Montpellier and among others, a professor who is a
specialist. Following their advice, my father entered a
hospital in that town in order to have an operation.
At the end of six days treatment, the doctor declared
that it would be difficult to perform an operation, two
persons with the same malady having died under the
operation, and that there was no other remedy. In
answer to my earnest questions, he replied that the
swelling would keep on increasing until finally it would
suffocate him. Think, Mother Superior, what terrible
news!

We returned to Cette, very sad, but without being
discouraged. We still had faith and knew that all is
possible with God. We made a Novena to Our Lady of
Lourdes, who did not wish to cure our father but to
let Marie Celine have the honor of doing so, for on the
last day of the Novena to Celine, at the very time when
we were saying the prayers, *we were heard.* The
swelling, breaking externally, entirely disappeared, and
my father is quite well again.

The cure was so evident that all who had seen our

patient declared that *it was a miracle.* You may publish this. He was given up by a *number of doctors* and was threatened with death by suffocation, so what gratitude do we not owe Marie Celine! I am going to be her apostle. This morning I made her known to a Curé of the town; yesterday to Foujet at Marseilles; last week to Benzois at Loire; not to mention Montpellier where I do nothing but speak of her. I have chosen her for my patroness in my difficulties.   —Rose Broue

Mons
October, 1909

A young girl at Mons was suffering from some gastric trouble. For three months she had not been able to eat or digest her food and suffered agonizing pains. After making a Novena through the intercession of Marie Celine and wearing with confidence a sachet containing a piece of her clothing, this young girl *obtained a cure* which she attributes to the intercession of the dear little Saint whose name she has the happiness to bear.

Valenciennes
July 18, 1922

My son-in-law had been ill for some time, and seeing no signs of recovery, I thought of Sister Marie Celine. I send you herewith an offering in thanksgiving for this *cure,* which was granted *as soon as the relic was applied to the patient.*   —S. Magniez

Nantes
November 22, 1922

For some time I have had a good deal of suffering from a weak stomach. During more severe attacks I have had to seek relief by means of powders prescribed by the medical facility. Sometimes one of these is sufficient, at other times several have to be taken in succession. I have known myself to take as many as seven at intervals within twenty-four hours.

Last night about ten o'clock I was troubled with one of these attacks. I took three of the powders in succession and slept till shortly after midnight. But then, alas, the trouble returned. I had wished especially to go to Holy Communion in the morning as it was the Feast of Our Lady's Presentation in the Temple.

I had therefore to make up my mind, "Can I do without another powder or not?" Suddenly the thought of Sister Celine crossed my mind. I addressed her in words of this kind: "Little Sister, as today is the Feast of Our Lady's Presentation, I am anxious to hear Mass and receive Holy Communion; but if this pain does not diminish through your help, I shall be obliged to break my fast." *As soon as I had said this I obtained relief.* I fell asleep and did not awake until 5:30, when I got up *without any pain.*

—General Comte Cornulier de Lucinere

Estavayer-de-Lac, Switzerland
January 7, 1923

I write these lines to ask you to join with us in thanking Sister Marie Celine. Here are two of the *favors* obtained through her intercession. One of our orphan girls five-and-a-half years old, had a sore knee. It was so swollen that the girl could not stand. The Doctor thought it was a tumor and put her to bed. In the meantime we had read the Life of Sister Marie Celine, and as she had suffered when young, one of our Sisters said, "We must pray to Sister Marie Celine to cure Cecile." The Sisters and the children prayed so well that *two days later the knee was normal,* the girl could stand and even walk. She has had no more pain in it for the last two years.

The second *favor* was this: Two of our orphans were going to be taken away from our care and placed with Protestants for the sake of economy. Humanly speaking we could not do anything to prevent it, so we applied again to our dear Sister Marie Celine by means of a fervent Novena made by the children and several Sisters.

To our great joy things were settled by the person who had previously been our chief opponent, and the two children remained with us.

Our best thanks to our heavenly advocate.

—Cesarine Cachard, Sister of Charity

Two pious travellers, praying at the tomb of Marie Celine, were conscious of a delicious odor which they inhaled for a long time, their foreheads pressed against the tombstone.   —(Related by M. l'Abbe Biguer)

Sandancourt
August 12, 1910

When I received the portrait of Marie Celine and
the little sachets which I always keep with me, I was
surprised at the perfume coming from them.

Now that I have devoutly read and re-read the mar-
vels and miracles worked by the intercession of your
beloved Sister Celine, I understand whence came this
sweet perfume which at once gave me confidence.

—Madame Laurent

Paris
April 29, 1911

I put on a relic of Marie Celine and went out to say
some prayers in the parish church, although the state
of my health excused me from going out of doors. As
soon as I entered the church, exquisite perfumes surrounded me and I felt very happy with a supernatural
happiness. I could hardly believe it, not daring to think
that such a favor should be accorded to me. Everywhere I went these sweet odors followed me, and I
observed that there were no flowers in the vicinity.

—Mdlle. Charlotte Bouchard

November, 1922

The Mother Superior of the Little Sisters of the Poor
at Sous-le-Bois, Nord, was lately complaining to Marie
Celine, "My dear little Saint, for a long time you have

given me no sensible proof of your kind protection." Shortly afterwards her room was filled with a fragrance which could not be accounted for by any natural cause. All the Nuns were present at the time, and each one perceived a different perfume—rose, lily, violet, etc.

Cure of a Baby dying of double bronchopneumonia with suffocating catarrh and danger of asphyxia.

I, the undersigned, mother of the child, Marie-Sophie L____, certify before God as follows:

On December 28, 1942, my daughter, born on November 15, was suddenly taken ill with severe bronchialpneumonia. I hurriedly called our parish priest to administer the Sacrament of Baptism. I then called in Doctor C____, a specialist in children's diseases, to assist our two local doctors.

Day and night my mother, and the servant and I, kept watch over the baby, holding her in our arms. All those who saw the child were afraid to come back the next day, in case she should be dead.

On December 29, a friend of ours, Miss de L____ who had been informed, came to help us, bringing us a relic of Sister Marie-Céline, which we immediately fixed on the sick child. Then she asked the Convent of the Poor Clares for a novena in honor of Sister Marie Céline. We also joined in it.

During the night of December 29 and 30 my husband, seeing that all medical efforts had been unavailing, left the child thinking that she would not live more than a few hours, and he was astounded to find her alive at 7 a.m. on December 30.

The days of December 30 and 31 were still full of anxiety. But this ceased on the morning of January 1, 1943. Our daughter was saved.

No one in the household doubts that the cure was due to the intercession of Sister Marie Céline on behalf of a little creature of which medical science had despaired.

—Yvette L. L____

B____, July 28, 1945

General Practitioner

Doctor L. L____

B____

I, the undersigned, Doctor L____ certify that from Monday, December 28, 1942 at midday, I treated the infant Marie-Sophie L____, who was suffering from double broncho-pneumonia with suffocating catarrh and danger of asphyxia.

This baby, which had been breast-fed by her mother, had not gained in weight for two weeks and at that time weighed less than six pounds, though she was one and a half months old.

Realizing at once the seriousness of her condition, I called in for consultation during the afternoon, Doctor C____, formerly chief of the children's clinic, who advised, in order to save the baby, her immediate removal to the clinic to put her in an oxygen tent.

My brother, Doctor J. L____, having been informed, arrived about 5 p.m. and, noticing the extreme weakness of the child, we decided not to remove her to the clinic, as she was not capable of withstanding the strain of the journey.

By means of repeated injections of solution of camphor the baby passed the night, continually in the arms of some member of the household at the fireside, with a little sugared water, or rather, a pad of cotton-wool soaked in this water, on her lips from time to time.

Next day, on Tuesday, December 29, the condition was unchanged—that is, of extreme gravity.

Injections of solution of camphor, warm wraps and oxygen were applied.

During the night of Tuesday, December 29 to Wednesday, December 30 about 2 a.m., having given up hope on seeing the child in the grip of asphyxia (she was breathing by gasps, with her mouth wide open and twisted to inhale a little air), I left the room to lie down on a sofa for a few hours, convinced that the illness was at its last stage, and that the child would be dead next time I saw it.

I was astounded when I came back to the bedroom at 7 a.m. to find that the baby had not only survived, but that she accepted a little milk diluted with water from a spoon.

At that point, my hopes having revived, I continued the prescribed treatment till, on the evening of December 30, I had the joy of seeing the baby at last close its eyes which had been wide open for more than 48 hours, and rest two good hours.

In conclusion, I can say that it was during that night of Tuesday to Wednesday that the situation which, on medical grounds appeared hopeless (the heart no longer reacted to the injections, the asphyxia was more acute than before), turned in favor of the child.

—B____, July 11, 1945
Doctor L. L.

July 10, 1945

Doctor G. C_____
Former Hospital Resident Specialist,
Former Head of the Clinic of Children's
   Diseases in the Faculty of Medicine

I, the undersigned, certify that I was called in consultation at the end of December, 1942 to the case of the child Marie-Sophie L_____ then aged a month and a half. This child, who was hypotrophical and weighed less than six pounds, exhibited symptoms of double broncho-pneumonia with catarrhal suffocation and danger of asphyxia, cardiac exhaustion, and seemed on the point of death. After having treated the child and prescribed a treatment for the day, I left the child, whom I considered would certainly die within the next few hours. One of my colleagues who had seen the child considered it useless to continue the treatment, and it was decided not to remove the baby to a clinic as I had required, owing to the danger involved in any movement.

Within 48 hours the situation which was almost desperate had changed, and the child was out of danger the third day.

Doctor G. C_____

PART FIVE

The Poor Clares Today

The Poor Clares Today

The Second Order of St. Francis, more commonly known as the Poor Clares, is a worldwide monastic Order of cloistered contemplative women present on all five continents. There are a total of about 900 autonomous monasteries belonging to the different branches of Poor Clares. Interestingly, Pope John Paul II noted in 2003: "Seven hundred and fifty years since Pontifical approval, the Rule of St. Clare maintains intact its spiritual fascination and theological richness. The perfect consonance of human and Christian values, the wise harmony of contemplative fervor and evangelical rigor makes it . . . a highway to follow, without compromises or concessions to the spirit of the world."

We, the Poor Clare Colettine Nuns, see in Blessed Marie Celine of the Presentation a shining example of fidelity to this Rule "without compromises or concessions to the spirit of the world." We strive to carry on an 800-year-old tradition, tested by time, which has been a secure way to holiness, a highway taken by many a saint.

If you are inspired by the following pages and wish to know more about this way of life, visit our websites, call us, or write to us. www.rockfordpoorclares.org www.poorclare.org (Click on *observances*, then *Poor Clare Colettines*.)

Reverend Mother Abbess
Corpus Christi Monastery
2111 South Main Street
Rockford, IL 61102-3591

(815) 963-7343

Reverend Mother Abbess
Annunciation Monastery
6200 East Minooka Road
Minooka, IL 60447-9458

(815) 467-0032

Other monasteries of similar observance:

Mary Mother of the Church
Monastery
2505 Stonehedge Dr.
Alexandria, VA 22306-2451

Bethlehem Monastery of Poor
Clares
Mount Saint Francis
5500 Holly Fork Rd.
Barhamsville, VA 23011-2209

Monastery of the Blessed
Sacrament
3501 Rocky River Dr.
Cleveland, OH 44111-2998

Immaculate Heart Monastery
of Poor Clares
28210 Natoma Rd.
Los Altos Hills, CA 94022-3220

Poor Clare Monastery of the
Immaculate Conception
12210 S. Will Cook Rd.
Palos Park, IL 60464

Monastery of Poor Clares
215 E. Los Olivos St.
Santa Barbara, CA 93105-3605

Monastery of St. Clare
200 Marycrest Dr.
St. Louis, Mo 63129-4813

St. Joseph Monastery of Poor
Clares
P.O. Box 160
1671 Pleasant Valley Rd.
Aptos, CA 95001-0160

Monastery of Our Lady of
Mercy
300 N. 60th St.
Belleville, IL 62223-3927

Maria Regina Mater
Monastery
1175 N. County Rd. 300 W.
Kokomo, IN 46901-1799

Monastery of Our Lady of
Guadalupe
809 E. 19th St.
Roswell, NM 88201-7514

Saint Clare's Monastery
421 S. 4th St.
Sauk Rapids, MN 56379-1898

Klooster Maria Moeder Van
Der Kerk
Sint Claralaan 1
NL-5654 AS EINDHOVEN, NB
NEDERLAND (Netherlands)

Photos from the Daily Life
of the Poor Clares
of Rockford, Illinois

Above: On her "Clothing" day the postulant, dressed as a bride—the "Bride of Christ"—approaches the altar in a ceremony to receive the habit of the Order.

Left: The Sisters congratulate the newly clothed novice. She will wear a white veil until her Profession, when she will receive the black veil.

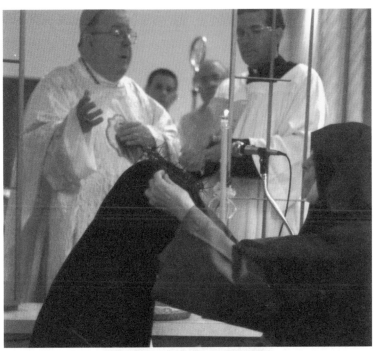

At solemn Profession the Poor Clare makes final perpetual vows and receives a crown of thorns, identifying her with her Crucified Spouse in a life of sacrificial love.

Every year, on the anniversary of her solemn profession, each Sister makes a devotional renewal of vows. In a public ceremony before the community, she places her hands in the hands of the Mother Abbess to renew the gift of herself before the altar.

A Poor Clare nun reads in her cell. When she dies, the crucifix on the wall will be placed in her hands and the crown of thorns will be put into the coffin by her side. A wreath of fresh white flowers will be placed on her head.

Novenas and other prayers are offered for friends, relatives and
benefactors and for those who call and request prayers.

The Sisters pray the Liturgy of the Hours, also called the Divine Office, in choir. Since they pray the Divine Office, which is the official prayer of the Church, the Poor Clares are properly called "nuns" as well as "Sisters."

Left: The Blessed Sacrament exposed in the choir chapel. The Sisters are privileged to have daily private exposition of the Blessed Sacrament in the choir of the cloister.
Lower: The Blessed Sacrament exposed in the public chapel.

A Sister prays in the choir chapel.

163

The exterior of the Poor Clares' Corpus Christi Monastery in Rockford, Illinois. The monastery was founded in 1916. The arched doorway leads to the public chapel, where visitors may attend Mass every morning at 7:00.

A monthly day of recollection, called "Recluse Day" in honor of St. Colette, is spent in even greater silence and solitude than usual, as ordinary duties are set aside for the day. Here a Sister enjoys the solitude of the rooftop for her spiritual reading.

164

Above: A visit to a Marian shrine on the grounds. Devotion to Mary and the imitation of her virtues have a special place in Poor Clare spirituality.

Left: A Poor Clare tends the garden. The monastery garden produces vegetables for meals and flowers for the altar.

The Poor Clares remember their departed Sisters in prayer and make a daily visit to the cemetery on the monastery grounds during November, the month of the faithful departed.

Above: Meals at the monastery are taken in silence while listening to spiritual reading, taped conferences, or the biography of a saint.
Below: The recreation period is a joyful time to work together on some community project and to enjoy conversation together.

Formation classes are given in the novitiate to postulants, novices and junior professed Sisters.

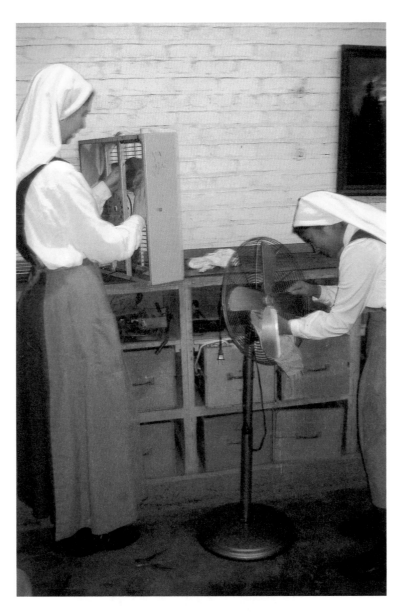

Postulants are initiated into the household maintenance tasks.

Above: Repairing the roof of a shed.
Below: Preparing food for the community. The Poor Clares observe a perpetual fast and abstinence, so their diet consists primarily of carbohydrates, fruits and vegetables. Twice a week the Sisters eat fish.

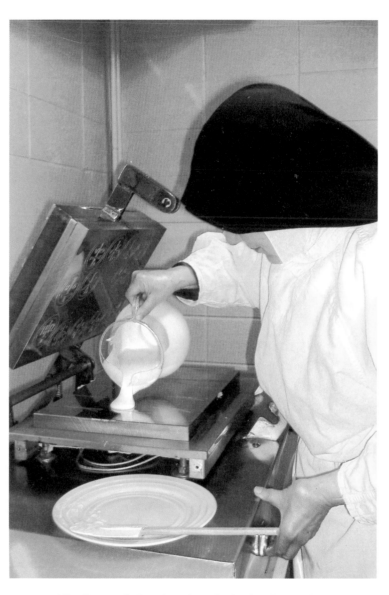

The Sisters bake altar breads for local parishes.

Upper left: The Sisters sew vestments and First Communion veils to help support themselves. *Upper right:* Preparing food. *Lower:* Cards and announcements are printed on an old press. Printing in one form or another is a monastic tradition dating back to the Middle Ages.

Novices and professed Sisters pray before a picture of Blesed Marie
Celine of the Presentation.

The Sisters praying in procession. A statue of St. Francis of Assisi, one of their founders, is visible in the background. The Sisters also honor St. Clare and St. Colette as their founders.

174

Prayer to Obtain Favors through the Intercession of Marie Celine of the Presentation

O LORD JESUS, we beseech Thee, through Thy predilection for the humble, the little ones and the poor, vouchsafe to glorify Thy faithful servant Marie Celine, and once more to fulfill the words of Thy divine Mother in her admirable canticle: "He hath exalted the humble."

O MOST LOVING JESUS, we ardently implore of Thee—if it be for Thy glory and for the sanctification of souls—deign to glorify Thy humble servant, and let her come to our assistance by obtaining the favors we beg through her intercession. Amen.

Nihil Obstat: Imprimatur:
C. Schut, D. D.   Edm. Can. Surmont
Censor deputatus   Vic. Gen.
      Westmonasterii, die 14 Mai, 1923

Persons receiving favors attributed to the intercession of Blessed Marie Celine are asked to inform the Poor Clares, Monastere Ste. Claire, 2, Avenue de la Rochelle, 17137 NIEUL SUR MER, France.

The Poor Clares of Nieul sur Mer shall be most grateful to any who are willing to send an offering to help toward the expenses of the Cause of Sister Marie Celine in Rome.

"In Heaven I will forget no one . . ."
—*Blessed Marie Celine of the Presentation*

If you have enjoyed this book, consider making your next selection from among the following . . .

At your Bookdealer or direct from the Publisher.

Toll-Free 1-800-437-5876   **Fax 815-226-7770**
Tel. 815-226-7777   **www.tanbooks.com**
Prices subject to change.